with CD-ROM/
Audio CD

face2face

Starter Student's Book

Chris Redston
with Gillie Cunningham

Contents

Listening	Help with Listening and Help with Sounds	Speaking	Writing
Conversations at a party Phone numbers		Names Introducing people Phone numbers	
Where are you from?	**Help with Listening** word stress	Names and countries What's his / her name? Where's he / she from?	Sentences about famous people
Welcome to the class		First names and surnames Conversations in class	
	Help with Sounds /æ/ and /ə/	Talking about a photo	
			Reading and Writing Portfolio 1 WB p60
Around the world		True or false?	True and false sentences
Photos of friends		About your partner Ben's friends	*yes / no* questions
At an employment agency		Good morning! Interview your partner	Filling in a form
How old is your cat?	**Help with Listening** numbers with *-teen* and *-ty* **Help with Sounds** /ɪ/ and /iː/	Questions with *How old … ?* Guess the ages	
			Reading and Writing Portfolio 2 WB p62
	Help with Listening contractions	Talking about the two emails	
Fiona's family Our grandchildren		Your family	Sentences about Fiona's family
Prices Two customers in a café		Ordering food and drink in a café	
They love chocolate!	**Help with Sounds** /ɒ/ and /ʌ/	Food and drink	Sentences with *love, like, eat, drink, a lot of*
			Reading and Writing Portfolio 3 WB p64
Life in Peru and Australia		True or false?	True and false sentences
An online interview	**Help with Listening** questions with *do you*	Your free time Your partner's free time	Your free time *yes / no* questions
Four conversations in a shop		Buying things in a shop	A conversation in a shop
Times	**Help with Sounds** /θ/ and /ð/	Film times	
			Reading and Writing Portfolio 4 WB p66
Carol's routine		Your daily routine Your partner's daily routine	
Lunch on Monday	**Help with Listening** sentence stress (1)	Your best friend	Questions with *does*
Conversations in a restaurant	**Help with Listening** sentence stress (2)	Ordering food and drink in a restaurant	A conversation in a restaurant
Sunday routines	**Help with Sounds** /w/ and /v/	Your Sunday routine	True and false sentences
			Reading and Writing Portfolio 5 WB p68

Listening	Help with Listening and Help with Sounds	Speaking	Writing
Susan's home town		A town or city you know	Sentences with *there is / there are*
Welcome to my home	**Help with Listening** linking (1)	Places near Susan's flat Places near your home	Questions with *Is there a …?* and *Are there any … ?*
Conversations at a tourist information centre		Asking for information at a tourist information centre	
My favourite colour is pink	**Help with Sounds** /tʃ/ and /dʒ/	Your clothes and colours Favourite things and people	Questions with *your favourite*
			Reading and Writing Portfolio 6 WB p70

We're very different		Things you love, like, don't like and hate	Questions with *Does … like … ?* Questions with *Do you like … ?*
Help with the children	**Help with Listening** *can* or *can't*	Things you and your family can and can't do	True or false sentences with *can* and *can't* Questions with *can*
Three conversations in the street		Asking for and giving directions	
An Internet questionnaire	**Help with Sounds** /s/ and /ʃ/	Things you do online	
			Reading and Writing Portfolio 7 WB p72

Three amazing days		When I was ten	Sentences with *was* and *were*
An Indian wedding		When and where people were born Your last wedding or party	
Dates Happy birthday!	**Help with Listening** linking (2)	When's your birthday? Making suggestions	A conversation about next Saturday
Fantastic festivals	**Help with Sounds** /ɔː/ and /ɜː/	Festivals	
			Reading and Writing Portfolio 8 WB p74

	Help with Listening Present Simple or Past Simple	How you travel around The last time you visited a different town or city	Sentences in the Past Simple
Favourite places		Things Nancy and Jeff did on holiday Your last holiday	Things you do on holiday Past Simple questions
Two days in Liverpool	**Help with Listening** sentence stress (3)	Last weekend Buying train tickets	Sentences about last weekend
	Help with Sounds /l/ and /r/	Questions about you and your partner	*Wh-* questions
			Reading and Writing Portfolio 9 WB p76

A world language		Your future plans	Sentences with *be going to*
A new start		Questions with *be going to* Students' future plans	Questions with *be going to*
See you soon!		Saying goodbye and good luck	
			Reading and Writing Portfolio 10 WB p78

Phonemic Symbols p126   **Answer Key** p126   **Classroom Instructions** p127   **CD-ROM/Audio CD Instructions** p128

1 New friends

1A What's your name?

Vocabulary numbers 0–12
Grammar *I, my, you, your*
Real World saying hello;
introducing people; phone
numbers; saying goodbye

Hello!

1 **a)** R1.1 P Look at the photo. Read and listen to conversation 1. Listen again and practise.

TIP! • P = pronunciation

b) Practise conversation 1 with four students. Use your name.

c) Tell the class your name.

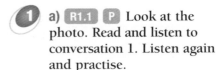

Hello, I'm Francesca.

Hello, my name's Lee.

2 **a)** R1.2 P Read and listen to conversation 2. Listen again and practise.

b) Practise conversation 2 with four students. Use your name.

Help with Grammar
I, my, you, your

3 **a)** Fill in the gaps with *I* or *my*.

1 _I_ 'm Stefan.
2 _____'m fine, thanks.
3 _____ name's Emel.

b) Fill in the gaps with *you* or *your*.

1 How are _you_ ?
2 Nice to meet _____ .
3 What's _____ name?

G1.1 p101

4 R1.3 Listen and practise the sentences in **3**.

5 **a)** Fill in the gaps with *I, my, you* or *your*.

A

SUE   Hello, _my_ name's Sue. What's _____ name?
MARIO   Hello, _____'m Mario.
SUE   Nice to meet _____ .
MARIO   _____ too.

B

ADAM   Hi, Meg.
MEG   Hi, Adam. How are _____ ?
ADAM   _____'m fine, thanks. And _____ ?
MEG   _____'m OK, thanks.

b) R1.4 Listen and check.

c) Work in pairs. Practise the conversations in **5a)**.

①
STEFAN Hello, I'm Stefan. What's your name?
EMEL   Hello, my name's Emel.
STEFAN Nice to meet you.
EMEL   You too.

②
TIM   Hi, Anita.
ANITA   Hi, Tim. How are you?
TIM   I'm fine, thanks. And you
ANITA   I'm OK, thanks.

Introducing people

6 **a)** R1.5 P Read and listen to conversation 3. Listen again and practise.

b) Work in groups. Practise conversation 3. Use your names.

Numbers 0–12

7 **a)** R1.6 P Listen and practise these numbers.

0 zero	**5** five	**10** ten
1 one	**6** six	**11** eleven
2 two	**7** seven	**12** twelve
3 three	**8** eight	
4 four	**9** nine	

b) Work in pairs. Say four numbers. Write your partner's numbers. Are they correct?

Phone numbers

8 **a)** R1.7 P Read and listen to these questions and answers. Listen again and practise.

> What's your mobile number?
>
> It's 07954 544768.
>
> What's your home number?
>
> It's 020 7622 3479.

TIP! • In phone numbers 0 = *oh* and 44 = *double four*.

b) Work in pairs. Practise the questions and answers.

9 **a)** R1.8 Listen to three conversations. Write the phone numbers.

b) Work in pairs. Compare answers.

3

NINA	David, this is Polly.
DAVID	Hello, Polly. Nice to meet you.
POLLY	You too.

4

LUCY	Goodbye, Miki.
MIKI	Bye, Lucy. See you soon.
LUCY	Yes, see you.

Get ready ... Get it right!

10 Work in pairs. Student A → p86. Student B → p92.

Goodbye!

11 **a)** R1.9 P Read and listen to conversation 4. Listen again and practise.

b) Say goodbye to other students.

1B Where's she from?

Vocabulary countries
Grammar *he, his, she, her*
Real World *Where are you from?*
Help with Listening word stress
Review phone numbers; *I, my, you, your*

QUICK REVIEW ●●●
Write two phone numbers. Work in pairs. Say your phone numbers. Write your partner's numbers. Are they correct?

Countries

1 Look at the map. Match these countries to 1–12.

> Italy 7 Brazil Russia the USA
> Germany Egypt Australia Mexico
> Turkey the UK China Spain

Help with Listening Word stress

2 R1.10 Listen and notice the word stress (•) in the countries in **1**.
Italy Brazil

3 R1.10 P Listen again and practise.

4 Work in pairs. Look again at the map. Say a number. Your partner says the country.

> Number 7.   Italy.

Where are you from?

5 a) R1.11 Look at the photo of Stefan and Emel. Listen to the conversation and fill in the gaps.

b) R1.12 P Listen and practise.

c) Where are you from? Tell the class.

> I'm from Japan.   I'm from France.

> I'm from Colombia.   I'm from Moscow.

d) Work in groups. Ask other students where they are from.

EMEL   Where are you from, Stefan?
STEFAN I'm from .... And you?
EMEL   I'm from ....

What's his name?

6 **a)** Look again at the photo of Stefan and Emel. Match questions 1–4 to answers a)–d).

1 What's his name?   a) He's from Russia.
2 Where's he from?   b) His name's Stefan.
3 What's her name?   c) She's from Turkey.
4 Where's she from?   d) Her name's Emel.

b) **R1.13** **P** Listen and practise.

Help with Grammar *he, his, she, her*

7 **a)** Fill in the gaps with *he* or *his*.

1 What's _his_ name?
2 .... name's Stefan.
3 Where's .... from?
4 ....'s from Russia.

b) Fill in the gaps with *she* or *her*.

1 What's _her_ name?
2 .... name's Emel.
3 Where's .... from?
4 ....'s from Turkey.   **G1.2** p101

8 **a)** Work in pairs. Look at photos 1–6 of famous actors and actresses. Write sentences. Use these names and countries.

Juliette Binoche	Penélope Cruz	Will Smith
Jackie Chan	Nicole Kidman	Daniel Craig

France	Spain	the UK	China	the USA	Australia

1 *Her name's Juliette Binoche. She's from France.*

b) **R1.14** Listen and check.

9 Work in new pairs. Ask and answer questions about the people in the photos.

> What's her name?   Juliette Binoche.

> Where's she from?   France.

Get ready ... Get it right!

10 Work in pairs. Student A → p87. Student B → p93.

①    ②

③    ④

⑤    ⑥

1C In class

QUICK REVIEW ●●●
Work in pairs. Ask the names of students in your class:
A *What's his name?* **B** *Marcus. What's her name?* **A** *Ana.*

The alphabet

1 R1.15 **P** Listen and say the alphabet. Notice the **vowels** and the **consonants**.

Aa Bb Cc Dd Ee Ff Gg
Hh Ii Jj Kk Ll Mm Nn
Oo Pp Qq Rr Ss Tt Uu
Vv Ww Xx Yy Zz

2 R1.16 Listen and write the letters.

What's your first name?

3 **a)** Look at photo A. Then match the teacher's questions 1–3 to the student's answers a)–c).

1 What's your first name, please?	a)	Molina.
2 What's your surname?	b)	M–O–L–I–N–A.
3 How do you spell that?	c)	It's Pedro.

b) R1.17 Listen and check.

Kate

Pedro

4 **a)** R1.18 Listen to the teacher talk to two more students. Write their names.

b) Work in pairs. Compare answers.

5 **a)** R1.19 **P** Listen and practise the questions in 3a).

first name → What's your first name, please?

b) Ask three students the questions in 3a). Write their first names and surnames.

Things in your bag (1)

6 **a)** Look at photo B. Match these words to things 1–10.

> a bag *1*   a dictionary   an apple
> a pen   a pencil   a book   a notebook
> an iPod   a mobile   an umbrella

b) R1.20 **P** Listen and practise.

7 Work in pairs. Look again at photo B. Say a number. Your partner says the thing.

(Number 1.) (A bag.)

Help with Vocabulary *a and an*

8 Look at the words in **6a)**. Fill in the gaps with *a* or *an*.

● We use .... with nouns that begin with a **consonant** sound.
● We use .... with nouns that begin with a **vowel** sound.

V1.5 p100

9 Fill in the gaps with *a* or *an*.

1 ..*a*.. country
2 .... number
3 .... English dictionary
4 .... student
5 .... answer
6 .... phone number

Excuse me!

10 **R1.21** Look at photo C. Listen to three conversations in class. Match students 1–3 to the words they ask about a)–c).

1 Magda   a) Brazil
2 Pedro   b) answer
3 Hasan   c) pencil

Real World Classroom language

11 **R1.21** Listen again. Tick (✓) these sentences when you hear them.

> Excuse me.
> What does (answer) mean?
> I'm sorry, I don't understand.
> What's (lápiz) in English?
> Can you repeat that, please?
> I'm sorry, I don't know.
> How do you spell (Brazil)?

RW1.7 p101

12 **R1.22** **P** Listen and practise the sentences in **11**.

C

Kate
Pedro
Magda
Hasan

13 **a)** Fill in the gaps with these words.

> Excuse   sorry   mean   spell   repeat   What's   understand   know

A

PEDRO   [1]*Excuse* me. What does 'notebook' [2].................. ?
KATE   Look. This is a notebook.

B

KATE   Do exercise 4 on page 10.
MAGDA I'm sorry, I don't [3].................. . Can you [4].................. that, please?
KATE   Do exercise 4 on page 10.

C

KATE   What's the answer to question 2?
HASAN   I'm [5].................. , I don't [6].................. .

D

PEDRO   [7].................. 'numero' in English?
KATE   Number.
PEDRO   How do you [8].................. that?
KATE   N–U–M–B–E–R.

b) Work in pairs. Practise the conversations. Take turns to be the teacher.

1D People and things

QUICK REVIEW ● ● ●
Write four English words. Work in pairs. Spell your words to your partner. Write your partner's words. Is your spelling correct?

1 **a)** Look at the picture. Match these words to people a)–e).

a baby *a)*　a boy　a girl　a man　a woman

b) **R1.23** **P** Listen and practise.

2 **a)** Look at the photo of Kate. Match these words to things 1–7.

a diary *4*　a chair　a table　a computer　a camera　a watch　a sandwich

b) **R1.24** **P** Listen and practise.

c) Work in pairs. What things from lesson 1C are in the photo?

3 **a)** Look at the photo of Kate for one minute. Close your book. Write all the things in the photo you can remember.

b) Work in pairs. Compare answers and check your partner's spelling. Who has more words?

Help with Vocabulary　Plurals

4 Look at these words. Write the missing letters.

SINGULAR	PLURAL
	+ -s
a chair	chairs
a table	tables
a thing	thing _
a boy	boy _
	+ -es
a watch	watches
a sandwich	sandwich _ _
	y → -ies
a diary	diaries
a baby	bab _ _ _
	irregular
a man	men
a woman	women
a person	people

V1.8 p100

5 **R1.25** **P** Listen and practise the plurals in **4**.

6 Write the plurals.

1　a girl *girls*　　6　a computer
2　a camera　　　　7　a woman
3　a country　　　　8　an apple
4　a watch　　　　　9　a dictionary
5　a man　　　　　　10　a person

7 Work in pairs. Look at p98.

1 a) R1.26 Look at the pictures. Listen to the sounds and words.

/æ/ 　　　/ə/

bag

computer

b) P Listen again and practise.

2 a) R1.27 Listen to these words. Notice how we say the pink and blue letters.

/æ/ bag　man　apple　practise
vocabulary　that　Japan
understand　camera　alphabet

/ə/ computer　woman　teacher
Italy　China　Brazil　Japan
understand　camera　alphabet

b) P Listen again and practise.

3 a) R1.28 P Listen to these sentences. Listen again and practise.

1 Is your camera from China?
2 Your apples are in my bag.
3 Practise the alphabet.
4 My computer is from Japan.
5 Is he from Italy or Brazil?
6 Is your teacher a man or a woman?

b) Work in pairs. Practise the sentences.

1 Review 　Language Summary 1, p100

1 a) Fill in the gaps with *I*, *my*, *you* or *your*. G1.1

ANDY　Hello, ¹*I*'m Andy. What's ²............. name?

KARA　Hello, ³............. name's Kara.

ANDY　Nice to meet ⁴............. .

KARA　⁵............. too.

BILL　Hi, Vicky.

VICKY　Hi, Bill. How are ⁶............. ?

BILL　⁷............. 'm fine, thanks. And ⁸............. ?

VICKY　⁹............. 'm OK, thanks.

b) Work in pairs. Practise the conversations. Use your name.

2 Write the numbers. V1.1

0 z e r o　　7 s _ _ _ _
5 f _ _ _　　12 t _ _ _ _ _
4 f _ _ _　　9 n _ _ _
6 s _ _　　　3 t _ _ _ _
2 t _ _　　　8 e _ _ _ _
1 o _ _　　　11 e _ _ _ _ _

3 Write the countries. V1.2

1 alytl　　I *taly*
2 suiRas　R.............
3 ceMiox　M.............
4 myranGe　G.............
5 niCah　　C.............
6 azrliB　　B.............
7 kueTyr　T.............
8 piSna　　S.............

4 a) Fill in the gaps with *he*, *his*, *she* or *her*. G1.2

A What's ¹*his* name?
B ²............. name's Andy.
A Where's ³............. from?
B ⁴............. 's from the UK.

A What's ⁵*her* name?
B ⁶............. name's Kara.
A Where's ⁷............. from?
B ⁸............. 's from the USA.

b) Work in pairs. Practise the conversations.

c) Work in new pairs. Ask the questions in 4a) about students in your class.

5 Write the vowels (*a, e, i, o, u*) in these things. Then put *a* or *an* in the boxes. V1.4 V1.5

1 a　b a g
2 □　_ ppl _
3 □　d _ ct _ _ n _ ry
4 □　_ mbr _ ll _
5 □　m _ b _ l _
6 □　n _ t _ b _ _ k
7 □　p _ nc _ l
8 □　_ P _ d
9 □　p _ n
10 □　b _ _ k

6 a) Find 12 things or people (→ ↓). V1.6 V1.7

W	O	V	B	O	Y	N	W
D	F	M	A	N	C	E	A
E	D	L	B	B	H	I	T
S	I	A	Y	G	A	R	C
S	A	N	D	W	I	C	H
H	R	G	A	W	R	A	K
J	Y	G	I	R	L	M	Y
C	O	M	P	U	T	E	R
P	T	A	B	L	E	R	Z
I	E	L	W	O	M	A	N

b) Write the plurals. V1.8

boy → boys

Progress Portfolio

a) Tick (✓) the things you can do in English.

□ I can say hello and goodbye.
□ I can ask people's names.
□ I can introduce people.
□ I can say phone numbers.
□ I can say where people are from.
□ I can say the alphabet.
□ I can say when I don't understand.
□ I can ask people to repeat things.
□ I can use plurals.

b) What do you need to study again? See CD-ROM ● 1A–D .

2 All about you

2A She's British

Vocabulary nationalities
Grammar *be* (singular): positive and negative
Review plurals; countries; *my, your, his, her*

QUICK REVIEW ●●●
Write five singular words (*a watch*, etc.). Work in pairs. Take turns to say your words. Say the plurals of your partner's words: **A** *a watch*. **B** *watches*.

Nationalities

 a) Write the missing vowels (*a, e, i, o, u*) in these countries.

1 *I* t a l y	5 G _ r m _ n y	9 T _ r k _ y
2 B r _ z _ l	6 _ g y p t	10 the _ K
3 R _ s s _ _	7 _ _ s t r _ l _ _	11 S p _ _ n
4 the _ S _	8 M _ x _ c _	12 C h _ n _

b) Match these nationalities to the countries in **1a)**.

a) German 5	e) American	i) British
b) Mexican	f) Spanish	j) Turkish
c) Italian	g) Egyptian	k) Chinese
d) Russian	h) Brazilian	l) Australian

 a) [R2.1] [P] Listen and practise the countries and nationalities.

Italy   Italian

b) Work in pairs. Say a country. Your partner says the nationality.

(the UK)   (British)

c) What's your nationality? Tell the class.

(I'm Japanese.)   (I'm French.)   (I'm Colombian.)

Around the world

 a) Work in pairs. Look at photos A–D. Fill in the gaps with a nationality from **1b)**.

b) [R2.2] Listen and check.

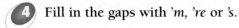 **Help with Grammar** *be* (singular): positive

4 Fill in the gaps with *'m*, *'re* or *'s*.

POSITIVE (+)
1 I .... British.	(= I am)
2 You *'re* a student.	(= you are)
3 He .... Chinese.	(= he is)
4 She .... Brazilian.	(= she is)
5 It .... American.	(= it is)

[G2.1] p103

Hi, my name's Karen. I'm ....

His name's Han Ming. He's ....

Her name's Paula. She's ....

I'm Alfredo and this is my car. It's ....

5 R2.3 P Listen and practise the sentences in 4.

I'm → I'm British.

6 **a)** Fill in the gaps with *'m* or *'s*.

1 She *'s* from São Paulo and she .... a student.
2 I .... from London and I .... a teacher.
3 It isn't a Mercedes. It .... a Chrysler.
4 She isn't Australian. She .... from the UK.
5 He isn't from Beijing. He .... from Shanghai.
6 I'm not American. I .... from Havana, in Cuba.

b) Work in pairs. Compare answers. Then match the sentences to photos A–D.

Help with Grammar *be* **(singular): negative**

7 Look again at **6a)**. Then fill in the gaps with *'m not*, *aren't* or *isn't*.

NEGATIVE (–)

1 I .... American.   (= am not)
2 You *aren't* a teacher.   (= are not)
3 He .... from Beijing.   (= is not)
4 She .... Australian.
5 It .... a Mercedes.

G2.2 p103

8 R2.4 P Listen and practise the sentences in 7.

I'm not → I'm not American.

True or false?

9 **a)** Check these words with your teacher.

the capital (city)   a singer   a company

b) Work in pairs. Look at photos 1–10. Tick (✓) the true sentences. Make the other sentences negative. Write the correct sentences.

1 Ankara is the capital of Turkey. ✓
2 Tiger Woods is British.
   Tiger Woods isn't British. He's American.
3 Cameron Diaz is Spanish.
4 Nintendo is a Japanese company.
5 Cairo is the capital of Egypt.
6 Big Ben is in New York.
7 Kylie Minogue is American.
8 Robbie Williams is an Australian singer.
9 BMW is a German company.
10 Hollywood is in San Francisco.

c) Check on p126. Are your answers correct?

Get ready ... Get it right!

10 Work in new pairs. Write three true sentences and three false sentences.

JK Rowling is British.
Lacoste is a Russian company.

11 **a)** Work in groups of four. Read your sentences to the other pair. Are the other pair's sentences true or false?

JK Rowling is British.   I think that's true / false.

Yes, you're right. / No, you're wrong.

b) Tell the class two of your true sentences.

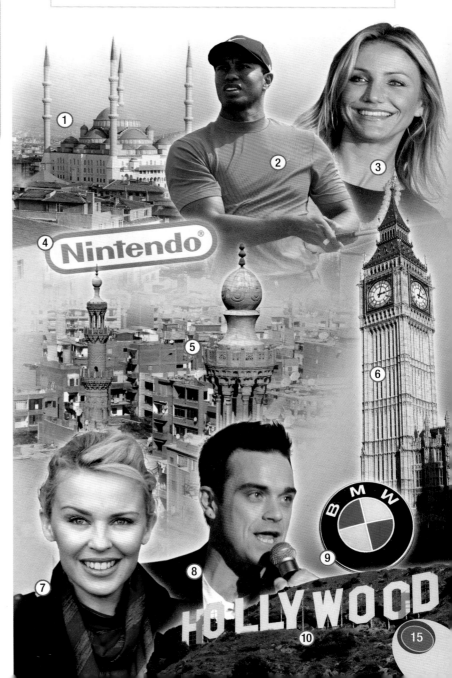

2B What's your job?

Vocabulary jobs
Grammar *be* (singular): questions and short answers
Review countries and nationalities; *be* (singular): positive and negative

QUICK REVIEW ● ● ●

Work in pairs. Take turns to say a country. Your partner says the nationality and a person or thing of that nationality: A *The UK*. B *British. James Bond is British*.

Jobs

1 **a)** Match these jobs to pictures a)–i).

a mánager *h)*   a dóctor   an áctor / an áctress
a shóp assistant   a téacher   a wáiter / a wáitress
a táxi driver   a musícian   a políce officer

TIP! ● In these vocabulary boxes we only show the main stress in words and phrases.

b) **R2.5** **P** Listen and practise.

c) Work in pairs. Ask questions about the people in pictures a)–i).

What's his job?   He's a waiter.

What's her job?   She's a waitress.

Photos of friends

2 **a)** Check these words with your teacher.

a friend   márried   síngle   beáutiful

b) **R2.6** Look at the photo of Amy and Ben. Listen and match these names to photos 1–4 on Amy's computer.

Claire   Steve   Daniela   Karl

c) Listen again. Complete the table.

	Karl	Steve	Claire	Daniela
country	*Germany*			
job	*a doctor*			

Help with Grammar
be (singular): *Wh-* questions

3 Fill in the gaps with *am*, *are* or *'s*.

WH- QUESTIONS (?)
1 Where ..*am*.. I?
2 Where .... you from?
3 Where .... he / she / it from?
4 What .... your name?
5 What .... his / her name?
6 What .... your job?
7 What .... his / her job?

G2.3 p103

4 **a)** **R2.7** **P** Listen and practise the questions in 3.

b) Cover the table in **2c)**. Work in pairs. Ask and answer questions about the people in photos 1–4.

What's his name?   Karl.

Where's he from?   Germany.

What's his job?   He's a doctor.

16

Ben

Amy

Is he a musician?

5 **a)** Look again at the table in **2c**).
Tick (✓) the correct answers.

1 Is Karl a musician?
   a) Yes, he is. **b)** No, he isn't. ✓
2 Is Steve from the USA?
   a) Yes, he is. **b)** No, he isn't.
3 Is Claire an actress?
   a) Yes, she is. **b)** No, she isn't.
4 Is Daniela Italian?
   a) Yes, she is. **b)** No, she isn't.
5 Are you from Russia?
   a) Yes, I am. **b)** No, I'm not.
6 Is your camera Japanese?
   a) Yes, it is. **b)** No, it isn't.

b) Work in pairs. Compare answers.

Help with Grammar *be* (singular):
yes / *no* questions and short answers

6 Fill in the gaps with *am, are, is* or *isn't*.

YES / NO QUESTIONS (?)	SHORT ANSWERS
_Am_ I in this class?	Yes, you are. / No, you aren't.
.... you from Russia?	Yes, I .... / No, I'm not.
.... he a doctor?	Yes, he is. / No, he ....
.... she Italian?	Yes, she .... / No, she isn't.
.... it Japanese?	Yes, it .... / No, it ....

G2.4 p103

7 R2.8 P Listen and practise the questions and short answers in **6**.

8 **a)** Fill in the gaps with *Is* or *Are*.

1 _Are_ you a student?
2 .... your teacher from the UK?
3 .... you Chinese?
4 .... you married?
5 .... your mobile in your bag?
6 .... you a manager?
7 .... Keira Knightley a musician?
8 .... Tom Cruise an actor?

b) Work in pairs. Ask and answer the questions. Use the correct short answers.

Are you a student?   Yes, I am.

Get ready ... Get it right!

9 Work in new pairs. Student A → p87.
Student B → p93.

2C Personal information

Vocabulary titles; greetings
Real World email addresses; personal information questions
Review jobs; *be* (singular): questions

QUICK REVIEW ● ● ●

Write four jobs. Work in pairs. Take turns to mime your jobs to your partner. Guess your partner's jobs: **A** *You're a doctor.* **B** *Yes, that's right.*

Good morning!

1 **a)** Match 1–3 to a)–c).

1	Mr (Brown)	a)	a married woman
2	Mrs or Ms (King)	b)	a single woman
3	Ms or Miss (Roberts)	c)	a man (married or single)

b) `R2.9` `P` Listen and practise.

Mr → Mr Brown

2 **a)** Look at pictures A–D. Complete the conversations with these phrases. Which three phrases mean *Hello*? Which phrase means *Goodbye*?

> Good morning   Good evening
> Good night   Good afternoon

b) `R2.10` `P` Listen and check. Listen again and practise.

c) Work in pairs. Practise the conversations.

Real World Email addresses

3 Look at this email address. Notice how we say . and @.

eve.smith@webmail.com

> eve **dot** smith **at** webmail **dot** com

`RW2.1` p103

William Brown
Manager

Brown and Forbes Ltd
8 Market Street
Bristol
BS3 7RJ

tel: 0117 927 6538
① email: william.brown@bfl.com

② Add contact   new email
Address:
frankmoon123@yahoo.com
Subject:
...od morning!

send   attach   copy   forward   print

③ To: annaroberts@webmail.net
④ Cc: katy.king6@hotmail.co.uk
Subject: How are you?

4 **a)** Work in pairs. Say email addresses 1–4.

b) `R2.11` Listen and check.

5 **a)** `R2.12` `P` Listen and practise email addresses 1–4.

@bfl.com → william.brown@bfl.com

b) Ask three students for their email addresses. Write the email addresses. Are they correct?

> What's your email address?   It's ...

Looking for a job

6 a) R2.13 Look at the photo. Listen to the interview and complete the form.

Tony
Amy

b) Work in pairs. Compare answers.

Real World Personal information questions

7 Fill in the gaps with *are* or *'s*.

1 What ..*'s*. your first name, please?
2 What .... your surname?
3 .... you married?
4 What .... your nationality?
5 What .... your address?
6 What .... your mobile number?
7 What .... your email address?

RW2.2 p103

8 R2.14 P Listen and practise the questions in **7**.

9 a) Work in pairs. Interview your partner and fill in the form.

b) Check your partner's form. Is it correct?

2D How old is she?

QUICK REVIEW ● ● ●
Write the numbers 0–12 in words (*zero, one,* etc.). Work in pairs. Check your partner's spelling. Say the numbers.

1 R2.15 P Listen and say these numbers.

13 thirteen   **16** sixteen   **19** nineteen
14 fourteen   **17** seventeen **20** twenty
15 fifteen   **18** eighteen

2 **a)** Match these words to the numbers.

~~thirty~~ ninety seventy forty sixty
eighty fifty a hundred

30 *thirty*   60 ....   90 ....
40 ....   70 ....   100 ....
50 ....   80 ....

b) R2.16 P Listen and practise.

Tony

Help with Listening **Numbers with *-teen* and *-ty***

3 **a)** R2.17 Listen to these numbers. Notice the stress.

fourteen forty sixteen sixty eighteen eighty

b) Where is the stress in these numbers?

seventeen ninety fifty thirteen
thirty nineteen seventy fifteen

c) R2.18 Listen and check.

4 R2.17 R2.18 P Listen again and practise.

5 **a)** Write the numbers.

21 *twenty-one*   24 ....   27 ....
22 *twenty-two*   25 ....   28 ....
23 ....   26 ....   29 ....

b) Work in pairs. Say these numbers.

27 35 49 52 68 73 86 94

6 **a)** Write four numbers.

b) Work in new pairs. Say your numbers. Write your partner's numbers. Are they correct?

7 **a)** Look at the photo. Match these words to 1–5.

a car *3*   a girl   a house   a cat   a dog

b) R2.19 Listen to five conversations. Fill in the gaps with the correct number.

1 The cat is ....
2 The house is .... years old.
3 The girl is ....
4 The car is .... years old.
5 The dog is ....

8 **a)** Fill in the gaps with these words.

~~How~~ is are I'm old

¹ *How* old ² .... your house?   It's 100 years ³............ .

How old ⁴ .... you?   ⁵ .... thirty.

b) R2.20 P Listen and check. Listen again and practise.

9 Work in pairs. Look again at the photo. Ask questions with *How old ... ?*.

10 Work in new pairs. Look at p98.

Help with Sounds /ɪ/ and /iː/

1 a) `R2.21` Look at the pictures. Listen to the sounds and words.

/ɪ/

six

/iː/

nineteen

b) `P` Listen again and practise.

2 a) `R2.22` Listen to these words. Notice how we say the pink and blue vowels.

| /ɪ/ | six thing his single Miss women British watches evening fifteen |

| /iː/ | nineteen he's she's people please Chinese police email evening fifteen |

b) `P` Listen again and practise.

3 a) Look at the vowels in **bold** in these words. Do we say /ɪ/ or /iː/?

it's /ɪ/ three /iː/ sandwiches
teacher think married isn't
read musician assistant me
Spanish Japanese sixteen

b) Work in pairs. Compare answers.

c) `R2.23` `P` Listen and check. Listen again and practise.

2 Review   Language Summary 2, p102

1 Write the nationalities. `V2.1`

Australia   Mexico   Italy
Russia   Germany   Brazil
the USA   Egypt   Spain
Turkey   the UK   China

Australia → *Australian*

2 Fill in the gaps with *'m, 're, 's, isn't, aren't* or *'m not*. `G2.1` `G2.2`

1 Libby *isn't* (–) from the USA, she *'s* (+) from the UK.
2 Ross .... (–) his first name, it .... (+) his surname.
3 I .... (–) from Colombia, I .... (+) from Mexico.
4 She .... (+) a Spanish teacher, but she .... (–) from Spain.
5 You .... (–) a teacher, you .... (+) a student.

3 Find eight jobs. `V2.2`

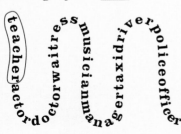

4 a) Make questions with these words. `G2.3`

1 name / your / 's / What ?
  What's your name?
2 you / Where / from / are ?
3 's / What / job / your ?
4 from / 's / Where / he ?
5 job / What / his / 's ?
6 What / name / 's / her ?
7 's / job / What / her ?

b) Match the questions in **4a)** to these answers.

a) I'm a doctor.
b) He's from Pisa, in Italy.
c) Her name's Evrim.
d) He's a waiter.
e) My name's Philip. *1*
f) She's an actress.
g) I'm from Australia.

5 a) Choose the correct words. `G2.4`

1 Are *you* / he a student?
2 *Is* / *Are* you from Spain?
3 Are *you* / *your* married?
4 *Is* / *Are* you from the capital of *you* / *your* country?
5 *Is* / *Are* your teacher British?
6 Is *you* / *your* mobile phone Japanese?

b) Work in pairs. Ask and answer the questions.

6 a) Write questions with *your* for these answers. `RW2.2`

1 It's Eve.
  What's your first name?
2 Smith.
3 I'm American.
4 It's 12 Lee Road, London, NW7 3EJ.
5 It's 07433 789215.
6 It's eve.smith@webmail.com.

b) Work in pairs. Ask and answer the questions in **6a)**. Answer for you.

7 Work in pairs. Say a number (0–100). Your partner says the next two numbers. `V2.5`

nineteen → *twenty, twenty-one*

Progress Portfolio

a) Tick (✓) the things you can do in English.

☐ I can say nationalities.
☐ I can ask and answer questions with *be*.
☐ I can talk about jobs.
☐ I can ask for and give personal information (name, address, etc.).
☐ I can say and understand numbers 0–100.
☐ I can talk about how old people are.

b) What do you need to study again? `2A–D`

3 People and places

3A Two cities

Vocabulary adjectives (1); word order with adjectives; *very*
Grammar *be* (plural): positive, negative, questions and short answers
Help with Listening contractions
Review numbers; *be* (singular)

QUICK REVIEW ●●●
Work in pairs. Count from 1 to 100 in threes: A *one*. B *four*. A *seven*.
Then count from 1 to 100 in fours: A *one*. B *five*. A *nine*.

Adjectives (1)

 a) Match the adjectives to pictures a)–h).

1	good $\boxed{d}$	bad
2	hot $\square$	cold
3	big $\square$	small
4	new $\square$	old
5	expensive $\square$	cheap
6	beautiful $\square$	ugly
7	friendly $\square$	unfriendly
8	nice $\square$	

b) `R3.1` `P` Listen and practise.

> **Help with Vocabulary** Word order with adjectives; *very*

 a) Read these rules about adjectives.

- Adjectives go after *be*: *Your watch is nice.*
- Adjectives go before nouns: *It's a new car.*
- Adjectives are **not** plural with plural nouns: *They're good friends.*

b) Match sentences a) and b) to pictures 1 and 2. Then read the rule.

 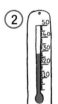

a) It's hot.
b) It's very hot.

- We put **very** before adjectives: *It's **very** hot.*

`V3.2` p104

 Make sentences with these words.

1 a / It's / computer / old / very .
   It's a very old computer.
2 a / He's / good / very / actor .
3 an / camera / It's / expensive .
4 very / nice / friends / are / His .
5 friendly / dogs / Your / very / are .

An email to friends

 a) Check these words with your teacher.

> a hotel   a room   a restaurant   an Internet café   near

b) Read email A. Where are Sally and Dan?

A

Hi Fiona and Nick

How are you? We're in Moscow! It's a beautiful city and the people are friendly, but it's very cold here. The restaurants are good and they aren't very expensive. We're in a new hotel near Red Square. The rooms are nice and they're very big. We aren't in the hotel now, we're in an Internet café. Where are you? Are you in London?
Love Sally and Dan

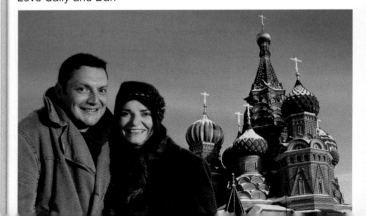

5 Read email A again. Tick (✓) the true sentences. Change the <u>adjectives</u> in the false sentences.

1 Moscow is a beautiful city. ✓
2 The people are ~~unfriendly~~. *friendly*
3 It's very hot in Moscow.
4 The restaurants are good.
5 Sally and Dan are in an old hotel.
6 The hotel rooms are nice.
7 The rooms are very small.

Help with Grammar
be (plural): positive and negative

6 Fill in the gaps with *'re* or *aren't*.

POSITIVE (+)

We _____ in a new hotel. (= we are)
You *'re* from the UK. (= you are)
They _____ very big. (= they are)

NEGATIVE (−)

We _____ in the hotel now. (= are not)
You *aren't* from Russia.
They _____ very expensive.

TIP! • *You* is singular and plural:
You're a student.
You're students.

G3.1 p105

7 R3.2 P Listen and practise the sentences in **6**.

Help with Listening Contractions

8 a) R3.3 Listen and fill in the gaps. You will hear each sentence twice.

1 We aren't *Italian* , we're _____ .
2 You're a very _____ _____ .
3 They're in a _____ _____ .
4 He's a _____ and he isn't _____ .
5 I'm an _____ and she's a _____ .
6 It's a _____ _____ _____ .

b) Work in pairs. <u>Underline</u> the contractions (*aren't*, *we're*, etc.) in **8a**).

c) Listen again. Notice the contractions.

Where are they?

9 Read email B. Choose the correct words.

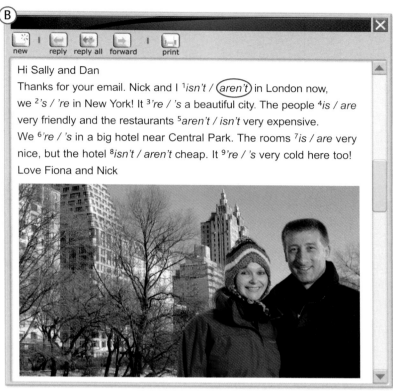

B

new reply reply all forward print

Hi Sally and Dan
Thanks for your email. Nick and I ¹*isn't / (aren't)* in London now, we ²*'s / 're* in New York! It ³*'re / 's* a beautiful city. The people ⁴*is / are* very friendly and the restaurants ⁵*aren't / isn't* very expensive. We ⁶*'re / 's* in a big hotel near Central Park. The rooms ⁷*is / are* very nice, but the hotel ⁸*isn't / aren't* cheap. It ⁹*'re / 's* very cold here too!
Love Fiona and Nick

10 Read email B again. Choose the correct answers.

1 Where are Fiona and Nick?
  a) London. b) New York.
2 Are they in a small hotel?
  a) Yes, they are. b) No, they aren't.
3 Are the rooms nice?
  a) Yes, they are. b) No, they aren't.

Help with Grammar
be (plural): questions and short answers

11 Fill in the gaps with *are* or *aren't*.

QUESTIONS (?)	SHORT ANSWERS
Are they in a small hotel?	Yes, they are. / No, they ....
.... you in London?	Yes, we .... / No, we aren't.
Where .... Fiona and Nick?	
Where .... you?	

G3.2 p105

12 R3.4 P Listen and practise the questions and short answers in **11**.

Get ready ... Get it right!

13 Work in pairs. Student A → p88. Student B → p94.

3B Brothers and sisters

Vocabulary family
Grammar possessive *'s*; subject pronouns (*I, you*, etc.) and possessive adjectives (*my, your*, etc.)
Review adjectives; jobs; *How old ...*

QUICK REVIEW ● ● ●
Write four adjectives. Work in pairs. Take turns to say an adjective from your list. Your partner says the opposite adjective: **A** *new.* **B** *old.* Then say one thing for each adjective: **A** *A new car.* **B** *An old computer.*

1. My name's Nick. Fiona's my **wife**. Kevin's our **son** and Anne's our **daughter**.

2. My name's Fiona. Nick's my **husband**. Anne and Kevin are our **children**.

3. My name's Kevin. Nick's my **father** and Fiona's my **mother**. Anne's my **sister**.

4. My name's Anne. Kevin's my **brother**. Fiona and Nick are my **parents**. I call them **mum** and **dad**.

Our family

1 **R3.5** Look at the photo of the Cooper family. Read and listen.

2 a) Complete the table with the words in **bold** in **1**.

♂ men / boys	♀ women / girls	♂♀ both
father (..............)	(mum)	....
....	daughter	.... (singular: **child**)
husband	....	
....	sister	

b) **R3.6** **P** Listen and practise.

3 Choose the correct words.

1 Nick is Fiona's *son* / (*husband.*)
2 Kevin is Nick's *brother* / *son*.
3 Fiona is Kevin's *mother* / *daughter*.
4 Anne is Fiona's *sister* / *daughter*.
5 Nick is Anne's *brother* / *father*.
6 Anne is Kevin's *mother* / *sister*.
7 Nick and Fiona are Kevin and Anne's *children* / *parents*.

Help with Grammar Possessive *'s*

4 Read the rule.

● We use a name (*Nick*, etc.) or a noun for a person (*sister*, etc.) + *'s* for the possessive. *Fiona is Nick's wife.* *It's my sister's car.*

TIP! ● *'s* can mean *is* or **the possessive**: *She's my sister.* (*'s* = *is*); *Kevin is Nick's son.* (*'s* = possessive).

G3.3 p105

5 **R3.7** **P** Listen and practise the sentences in **3**.

6 Make sentences about these people.

1 Nick → Kevin *Nick is Kevin's father.*
2 Fiona → Nick
3 Kevin → Fiona
4 Anne → Nick
5 Kevin → Anne
6 Anne and Kevin → Nick and Fiona

Our grandchildren

Mary

Sid

7 a) Look at the photo. Sid and Mary are Kevin and Anne's grandparents. Then complete the table with these words.

grandparents   grandson   grandmother

♂	grandfather	....
♀	....	granddaughter
♂♀	....	grandchildren

b) **R3.8** **P** Listen and practise.

8 a) **R3.9** Listen to Mary talk about her family. Put these people in the order she talks about them (1–5).

Sid *1*   Anne   Fiona   Kevin   Nick

b) Listen again. Answer these questions.

1 How old is Sid? *He's 64.*
2 What is Fiona's job?
3 How old is Fiona?
4 What is Nick's job?
5 Is Anne a good musician?
6 How old is Kevin?

Help with Grammar Subject pronouns (*I*, *you*, etc.) and possessive adjectives (*my*, *your*, etc.)

9 a) Look at these sentences. Then complete the table with the words in blue and pink.

I'm Mary and this is Sid, my husband.
Her husband's name is Nick and he's a doctor.
These are their two children – our grandchildren.
It's a very nice photo, I think.

subject pronouns	....	you	....	she	....	we	they
possessive adjectives	....	your	his	....	its	....	....

b) Are these words verbs (V) or nouns (N)?

> be *V*   sister *N*   family   listen   read   dog

c) Read these rules.

● We use subject pronouns with verbs (*I'm*, *you listen*, *they read*, etc.).
● We use possessive adjectives with nouns (*my sister*, *your family*, *their dog*, etc.).

G3.4 p105

10 Choose the correct words.

1 Is this *you* / *your* dictionary?
2 *They* / *Their* aren't with *they* / *their* parents.
3 This is *we* / *our* dog. *He* / *His* name is Prince.
4 *I* / *My* friend Tammy is from *you* / *your* city.
5 Are *you* / *your* at *he* / *his* house now?
6 *She* / *Her* brother's a musician, but *she* / *her* isn't.

Get ready ... Get it right!

11 Write the names of people in your family.

12 a) Work in pairs. Tell your partner about the people in your family. Ask questions about the people in your partner's family.

Lucas is my brother.
How old is he?
He's 32.
What's his job?
He's a manager.
Is he married?

b) Tell the class about one person in your partner's family.

Lucas is Pablo's brother. He's 32 and he's a manager. He's ...

Eat in or take away?

Vocabulary food and drink (1)
Real World money and prices;
How much ... ?; in a café
Review family; numbers

QUICK REVIEW ● ● ●
Write the name of a friend and the names of two people in his / her family.
Work in pairs. Tell your partner about your people. Ask questions if possible:
A *My friend's name is Liliana. She's 26.* B *What's her job?*

Money and prices

1 **a)** Match prices 1–6 to a)–f).

1	£10	a)	ten dollars
2	10p	b)	ten p (= pence)
3	£10.50	c)	ten euros
4	€10	d)	ten cents
5	$10	e)	ten (pounds) fifty
6	10c	f)	ten pounds

b) R3.10 P Listen and practise.

2 **a)** Work in pairs. Say these prices.

a £17 b 70p c $100 d €21 e 35c f $21.50 g €3.75 h £7.60

b) R3.11 P Listen and check. Listen again and practise.

3 **a)** R3.12 Listen to five conversations. Write the prices.

b) Work in pairs. Compare answers.

Real World *How much ... ?*

4 Fill in the gaps with *is* or *are*.

SINGULAR
1 How much .... this watch?
2 How much .... it?

PLURAL
3 How much .... the pens?
4 How much .... they?

RW3.2 p105

5 R3.13 P Listen and practise the questions in **4**.

Café Pronto

PRICE LIST

Hot drinks
coffee	£1.95
cappuccino	£2.30
espresso	£1.65
tea	£1.60

Cold drinks
mineral water	£1.25
Coke	£1.40
orange juice	£1.80

Food
croissant	£1.25
egg sandwich	£2.10
cheese and tomato sandwich	£2.45

Can I help you?

6 **a)** Look at the price list. Match the food and drink to photos 1–10.

b) R3.14 P Listen and practise the food and drink on the price list.

c) Work in pairs. Look again at photos 1–10. Test your partner.

What's number 1?   A cheese and tomato sandwich.

7 Look again at the price list. Work in new pairs. Choose food and drink. Ask your partner the price.

How much is an espresso and a croissant?   Two pounds ninety.

8 **a)** R3.15 Look at the photo of Café Pronto. Listen to two customers. Tick (✓) what they order on the price list.

b) Listen again. How much does each customer spend?

Real World *In a café*

9 Read the sentences. Fill in the gaps with these words.

> ~~help~~ very away please in

ASSISTANT

Can I ¹*help* you?

Sure. Anything else?

Eat in or take ³............ ?

OK, that's (£5.85), please.

You're welcome.

CUSTOMER

Yes, (two cappuccinos), please.

Yes, (a croissant), ²............ .
No, that's all, thanks.

Eat ⁴............ , please.
Take away, please.

Thank you ⁵............ much.
Thanks a lot.

> RW3.3 p105

10 **a)** R3.16 P Listen and practise the sentences in **9**.

b) Work in pairs. Practise the conversation in **9**. Take turns to be the customer.

11 **a)** Work in new pairs. Look again at the price list. Take turns to order food and drink.

b) Role-play a conversation for the class.

3D Bread and cheese

Vocabulary food and drink (2);
love, like, eat, drink, a lot of
Review money and prices;
food and drink (1)

QUICK REVIEW ● ● ●
Write four prices (*$55, £10.50*, etc.). Work in pairs. Say your prices.
Write your partner's prices. Are they correct?

1 a) Work in pairs. Look at the photo. Match these words to 1–16.

coffee *3*   milk   tea   sugar   meat   fish   orange juice   eggs
cheese   bread   pasta   rice   vegetables   fruit   chocolate   water

b) **R3.17** **P** Listen and practise.

2 a) Look at the photo for one minute. Remember the food and drink.

b) Close your books. Work in pairs. Say all the food and drink in the photo.

3 Match sentences 1–4 to pictures A–D.

1 I like fish. *B*   3 I drink a lot of coffee.
2 I love chocolate.   4 I eat a lot of rice.

4 **R3.18** **P** Listen and practise the sentences in **3**.

5 a) **R3.19** Listen to Fiona. Tick (✓) the food and drink in **1a)** she talks about.

b) Listen again. Choose the correct words.

1 Fiona and Nick love *coffee* / *milk*.
2 They drink a lot of *water* / *tea*.
3 They eat a lot of *meat* / *fish*.
4 Anne and Kevin like *eggs* / *cheese*.
5 They love *fruit* / *chocolate*.

6 a) Complete these sentences for you. Then write two more sentences about you.

1 I love ....
2 I like ....
3 I eat a lot of ....
4 I drink a lot of ....
5 ....
6 ....

b) Work in groups. Compare sentences.

Help with Sounds /ɒ/ and /ʌ/

1 a) R3.20 Look at the pictures. Listen to the sounds and words.

/ɒ/

/ʌ/

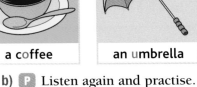

a coffee   an umbrella

b) P Listen again and practise.

2 a) R3.21 Listen to these words. Notice how we say the pink and blue vowels.

/ɒ/
coffee	dog	doctor	hot
watch	chocolate	orange
wrong	dollar	shop

/ʌ/
umbrella	much	number
country	mother	son	brother
husband	love	money

b) P Listen again and practise.

3 a) Cover 2a). Look at the vowels in **bold**. Which vowel sound is different?

1 h**o**t **o**range (m**u**ch)
2 m**o**ther d**o**ctor s**o**n
3 d**o**llar c**ou**ntry m**o**ney
4 d**o**g ch**o**colate l**o**ve
5 sh**o**p n**u**mber br**o**ther
6 w**a**tch h**u**sband wr**o**ng

b) Work in pairs. Compare answers.

c) R3.22 P Listen and check. Listen again and practise.

3 Review   Language Summary 3, p104

1 a) Write the vowels (a, e, i, o, u) in these adjectives.

1 g<u>o</u><u>o</u>d   4 ch _ _ p
2 b _ g   5 _ g l y
3 n _ w   6 c _ l d

b) Write the opposites of the adjectives in **1a)**. V3.1

1 good *bad*

2 a) Fill in the gaps with 's, 're, are, isn't or aren't. G3.1

Hi Ivan!
Eva and I ¹ *are* (+) at an English school in London! It ² .... (+) a good school, but it ³ .... (−) cheap. The teacher ⁴ .... (+) very good and the students ⁵ .... (+) friendly. We ⁶ .... (+) in a hotel near the school. The rooms ⁷ .... (+) nice, but they ⁸ .... (−) very big!
Love Olga

b) Make questions with these words. G3.2

1 are / Eva and Olga / Where ?
   Where are Eva and Olga?
2 cheap / Is / the school ?
3 the teacher / good / Is ?
4 Are / friendly / the students ?
5 's / the hotel / Where ?
6 big / Are / the rooms / very ?

c) Work in pairs. Ask and answer the questions in **2b)**.

3 Look at this family. Then fill in the gaps with the correct family word. V3.3

Simon ♂ + Mia ♀
Zara ♀   Harry ♂

1 Simon is Mia's *husband*.
2 Mia is Simon's ....
3 Zara is Mia's ....
4 Harry is Simon's ....
5 Zara is Harry's ....
6 Harry is Zara's ....
7 Simon is Zara's ....
8 Mia is Harry's ....

4 Look at these sentences. Does 's mean *is* or the possessive? G3.3

1 It's very cold. *'s = is*
2 Is this Lola's computer?
3 Where's Colin from?
4 Ali's a police officer.
5 It's my friend's car.
6 She's my son's teacher.

5 Write the possessive adjectives (*my*, etc.). G3.4

1 I *my*   5 it
2 you   6 we
3 he   7 they
4 she

6 a) Put this conversation in a café in order. RW3.3

ASSISTANT

a) OK, that's £3.20, please.
b) Can I help you? **1**
c) Eat in or take away?
d) Sure. Anything else?
e) You're welcome.

CUSTOMER

f) Thanks a lot.
g) Yes, an orange juice and an egg sandwich, please. **2**
h) Take away, please.
i) No, that's all, thanks.

b) Work in pairs. Practise the conversation. Take turns to be the customer.

Progress Portfolio

a) Tick (✓) the things you can do in English.

☐ I can use adjectives and *very*.
☐ I can understand a simple email.
☐ I can talk about families.
☐ I can talk about money and prices.
☐ I can understand a simple price list.
☐ I can buy food and drink in a café.
☐ I can talk about food and drink I like.

b) What do you need to study again? ● 3A–D

4 My world

4A I like it!

QUICK REVIEW ● ● ●
Write ten words for food and drink. Work in pairs. Compare lists.
Say which things you like on your partner's list: A *I like coffee.*

Vocabulary phrases with *like, have, live, work, study*
Grammar Present Simple (*I, you, we, they*): positive and negative
Review food and drink (1) and (2); family; *be*

Phrases with *like, have, live, work, study*

1 **a)** Match these words or phrases to the verbs.

> ~~football~~   two children   English   in a flat
> for a Spanish company   rock music   languages
> in the centre of the city   a car   in an office

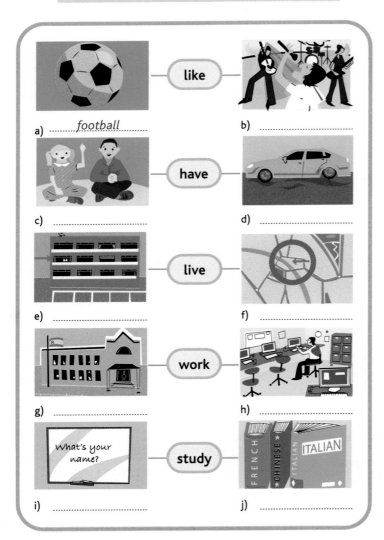

a) ...... *football* ......

b) ....

c) ....

d) ....

e) ....

f) ....

g) ....

h) ....

i) ....

j) ....

b) R4.1 P Listen and practise.

Life in Peru

2 **a)** R4.2 Read and listen to Ricardo. Who are
Cecilia, Carlos and Diego?

b) Read about Ricardo again. Choose the
correct words.

1 Ricardo is from (Peru) / Colombia.
2 He's *single / married*.
3 His flat *is / isn't* in the centre of Cuzco.
4 His car is *seven / nine* years old.
5 His sons *are / aren't* very good at English.
6 They like *Chinese / Japanese* food.

c) Work in pairs. Compare answers.

> My name's Ricardo and I'm from Cuzco, in Peru. I'm
> married and my wife's name is Cecilia. We live in a
> very nice flat in the centre of the city. I work for a
> car company, but I don't have a new car. My car is nine
> years old! We have two sons, Carlos and Diego, but we
> don't have a daughter. Carlos and Diego study English
> at school – they're very good. They like football, rock
> music and Chinese food, but they don't like homework!

Ricardo

Help with Grammar Present Simple (*I, you, we, they*): positive and negative

3 POSITIVE (+)

a) Underline the verbs in these sentences. They are in the Present Simple.

I <u>work</u> for a car company.
You study English.
We live in a very nice flat.
They like football.

TIP! • The Present Simple positive is the same for *I*, *you*, *we* and *they*.

NEGATIVE (–)

b) Look at these sentences. Notice the word order.

I	don't	have	a new car.	(don't = do not)
You	don't	study	German.	

c) Write these sentences in the table.

1 We **don't have** a daughter.
2 They **don't like** homework.

G4.1 p107

4 R4.3 P Listen and practise the sentences in **3**.

Life in Australia

5 **a)** Read about Sandra. Fill in the gaps with the positive (+) or negative (–) form of *like, have, live, work* or *study*.

b) R4.4 Listen and check.

6 **a)** Tick (✓) the sentences that are true for you. Make the other sentences negative.

1 I live in the centre of the city.
   I don't live in the centre of the city.
2 I work in an office.
3 I like Italian food.
4 I like rock music.
5 I have a computer.
6 I have a sister.
7 I study English.
8 I live in a small house.
9 I work for an American company.

b) Work in pairs. Compare sentences. How many are the same?

Get ready ... Get it right!

7 Write three true sentences and three false sentences about you. Use phrases from **1a)** or your own ideas.

I don't like Chinese food.
I live in a very small flat.
I work in a café.

8 Work in new pairs. Say your sentences. Are your partner's sentences true or false?

I don't like Chinese food.

I think that's true / false.

Yes, you're right. / No, you're wrong.

I ¹ *live* (+) in Melbourne, Australia, with my parents. We ² _____ (+) in a nice house near the centre of the city. I ³ _____ (+) two brothers, but I ⁴ _____ (–) a sister. My brothers ⁵ _____ (–) in Melbourne, they live in Sydney. I'm a manager and I ⁶ _____ (+) in an office near my house. In the evenings I ⁷ _____ (+) Japanese at a language school. I ⁸ _____ (+) Melbourne a lot, it's a beautiful city.

Sandra

4B · My free time

Vocabulary free time activities
Grammar Present Simple (*I, you, we, they*): questions and short answers
Help with Listening questions with *do you*
Review phrases with *like, have, live, work, study*

QUICK REVIEW ● ● ●
Complete four of these sentences for you: *I live ... , I have ... , I don't have ... , I work ... , I like ... , I don't like ...* . Work in pairs. Compare sentences. Are they the same? **A** *I live in a small flat.* **B** *Me too.*

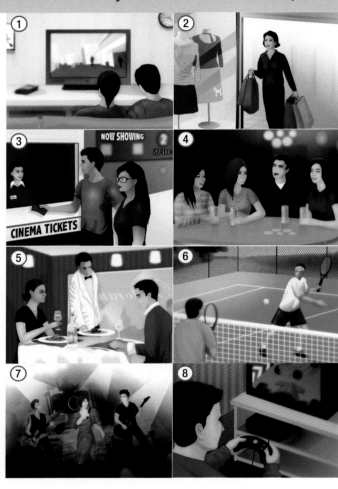

Free time activities

1 **a)** Match these phrases to pictures 1–8.

> go to concerts 7   go to the cinema   go shopping
> go out with friends   play tennis   watch TV or DVDs
> play computer games   eat out

b) R4.5 P Listen and practise.

2 **a)** Write four sentences about your free time. Use phrases from 1a).

I play tennis in my free time.
I watch TV a lot.
I don't go to concerts.

b) Work in pairs. Compare sentences.

An online interview

3 **a)** R4.6 Look at the web page on p33. Read and listen to the interview with Mike and Kim Black. Find three things they do in their free time.

b) Read the interview again. Are these sentences true (T) or false (F)?

1 Mike and Kim are married. *T*
2 They have a flat in London.
3 They don't like London.
4 They don't like U2.
5 They don't watch TV.
6 They go to concerts.
7 They don't like Mexican food.

Help with Grammar **Present Simple (*I, you, we, they*): questions and short answers**

4 **a)** Look at these questions. Notice the word order.

WH- QUESTIONS (?)

Where	do	you	live	in the UK?
What music	do	you	like?	

b) Write these questions in the table.

1 What **do** you **do** in your free time?
2 What food **do** you **like**?

TIP! ● Present Simple questions are the same for *I, you, we* and *they*.

c) Fill in the gaps with *do* or *don't*.

YES / NO QUESTIONS (?)	SHORT ANSWERS
Do you like London?	Yes, I do. No, I ....
.... you go to concerts?	Yes, we .... No, we don't.
.... they like Mexican food?	Yes, they .... No, they ....

G4.2 p107

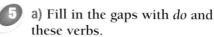

HOME   NEWS   INTERVIEWS   TICKETS   PHOTOS

THIS WEEK'S ONLINE INTERVIEW

**Today we talk to husband-and-wife rock stars
Mike and Kim Black from the British band Bad Day.**

Hi, Mike and Kim. Where do you live in the UK?
MIKE We have a flat in the centre of London.
KIM Yes, and we also have a house in Los Angeles.

Do you like London?
MIKE Yes, we do. It's a fantastic city, but it's very expensive.

What music do you like?
KIM Well, we listen to a lot of rock music, of course. We love the Red Hot Chili Peppers and U2.

What do you do in your free time?
MIKE We go out with friends when we're in London or LA.
KIM And we watch TV a lot, but we don't go to the cinema.

Do you go to concerts?
MIKE Yes, we do. Kim's brother is in a band called No Problem. We go to their concerts when we're in the UK.

And the last question. What food do you like?
MIKE We eat out a lot and we like Mexican food.
KIM Yes, and we love chocolate!

Thanks, Mike and Kim. Have a nice day!

5 a) Fill in the gaps with *do* and these verbs.

> live do like go have eat

1 Where _do_ Mike and Kim _live_ in the UK?
2 _____ they _____ a house in Los Angeles?
3 What _____ they _____ in their free time?
4 _____ they _____ to the cinema?
5 _____ they _____ out a lot?
6 _____ they _____ chocolate?

b) Work in pairs. Ask and answer the questions in **5a)**.

Help with Listening
Questions with *do you*

6 a) R4.7 Listen to these questions. Notice how we say *do you*.

1 Where do you /djə/ live?
2 What music do you /djə/ like?
3 Do you /djə/ go to concerts?
4 Do you /djə/ like Mexican food?

b) R4.8 Listen and write four questions with *do you*. You will hear each question twice.

c) Work in pairs. Compare sentences.

7 a) R4.9 P Listen and practise the questions in **6a)** and **6b)** and the short answers.

b) Work in pairs. Student A, ask the questions in **6a)**. Student B, ask the questions in **6b)**. Answer for you.

**Get ready ...
Get it right!**

8 Work in new pairs.
Student A → p86.
Student B → p92.

4C Buying things

Vocabulary things to buy; *this, that, these, those*
Real World in a shop
Review free time activities; money and prices; *How much … ?*

QUICK REVIEW ●●●
Work in pairs. Ask questions with *Do you …?* and find three things you both do in your free time: **A** *Do you play tennis?* **B** *Yes, I do. / No, I don't.*

Things to buy

1 **a)** Look at the pictures. Match these words to 1–10.

> a magazine *1*   a newspaper   a map   a postcard
> a birthday card   a box of chocolates   tissues
> sweets   batteries   chewing gum

b) R4.10 P Listen and practise.

c) Look again at the pictures. Test your partner.

(What's number 1?)   (A magazine.)

2 R4.11 Look at photos A–D. Listen and fill in the gaps with the correct prices.

Help with Vocabulary *this, that, these, those*

3 Look again at photos A–D. Then fill in the table with the words in **bold**.

	here ↓	there ↗
singular		
plural		

V4.4 p106

4 R4.12 P Listen and practise the questions in photos A–D.

this → *this map* → *How much is this map?*

How much is **this** map?
It's £_____ .

How much are **these** postcards?
They're _____p each.

How much is **that** box of chocolates?
It's £_____ .

How much are **those** batteries?
They're £_____ .

5 Fill in the gaps with *this*, *that*, *these* or *those*.

①
Are .... your postcards?

②
............'s my car!

③
What are .... ?

④
Is .... your newspaper?

Anything else?

6 **a)** **R4.13** Look again at photos A and B. Then listen to the conversations and fill in the gaps.

A

CUSTOMER Excuse me. Do you have any ¹ *maps* of London?

SHOP ASSISTANT Yes, they're over there.

C Thanks. How much is this map?

SA It's £4.75.

C OK. Can I have this map and these ² .... , please?

SA Sure. Anything else?

C No, that's all, thanks.

SA OK, that's ³£...................... , please. Thanks a lot. Bye.

C Goodbye.

B

C Hi. How much are these ⁴ .... ?

SA They're 50p each.

C OK, these ⁵...................... postcards, please. And can I have that box of chocolates?

SA Sure. Anything else?

C Yes, this birthday card, please.

SA OK, that's ⁶£...................... .

C Here you are.

SA Thanks very much. Goodbye.

C Bye.

b) Work in pairs. Compare answers.

Real World In a shop

7 **a)** Read these conversations. Fill in the gaps with these words.

~~Excuse~~	much	are	lot	else	have

CUSTOMER

¹ *Excuse* me. Do you have any (maps of London)?

SHOP ASSISTANT

Yes, they're over there.

How much is (this map)?

It's (£4.75).

How ² .... are (these postcards)?

They're (50p) each.

Can I ³ .... (that box of chocolates), please?

Sure. Anything ⁴ .... ?

Yes, this (birthday card), please.
No, that's all, thanks.

OK, that's (£10.65).

Here you ⁵ ....

Thanks a ⁶ ....
Thanks very much.

b) Read the conversations again. Find:

1 one question with *Do you have ... .*
2 one question with *Can I have ... .*
3 two questions with *How much ... .*

RW4.1 p107

8 **R4.14** **P** Listen and practise the sentences in **7a)**.

9 Work in pairs. Practise the conversations in **6a)**. Take turns to be the customer.

10 Work in the same pairs. Student A → p88. Student B → p94.

11 **a)** Work in new pairs. Write a conversation in a shop. Use language from **1a)** and **7a)**.

b) Practise the conversation until you can remember it.

c) Work in groups of four. Role-play your conversation for the other pair. What does the customer buy? How much does he / she spend?

4D Days and times

Vocabulary days of the week; time words
Real World telling the time; talking about the time
Review things to buy; numbers 0–100

QUICK REVIEW ● ● ●
Work in pairs. Write a list of things in the shop in lesson 4C. Check on p34. Which of these things do you have with you?

1 a) R4.15 P Listen and practise the days of the week.

Monday Tuesday Wednesday Thursday Friday Saturday Sunday

b) Work in pairs. Say a day. Your partner says the next two days.

> Friday

> Saturday, Sunday

c) Answer these questions.

1 What day is it **today**?
2 What day is it **tomorrow**?
3 What days are **the weekend**?

2 a) Put these time words in order.

> a day   a year 7   an hour   a second 1
> a month   a minute   a week

b) R4.16 P Listen and check. Listen again and practise.

c) Fill in the gaps with words in 2a). Use the singular or plural.

a) 60 _seconds_ = 1 minute
b) 60 .... = 1 hour
c) 24 .... = 1 day
d) 7 days = 1 ....
e) 365 days = 1 ....
f) 12 .... = 1 year

3 a) Match these times to clocks A–D.

> half past six C   quarter to seven   quarter past six   six o'clock

(A) (B) (C) (D)

b) We can say times in a different way. Match these times to clocks A–D.

> six A   six thirty   six forty-five   six fifteen

(a) 06:10   (e) 06:50
(b) 06:25   (f) 06:40
(c) 06:05   (g) 06:35
(d) 06:55   (h) 06:20

4 Match times 1–8 to clocks a)–h).

1 five past six c)   5 twenty-five to seven
2 ten past six   6 twenty to seven
3 twenty past six   7 ten to seven
4 twenty-five past six 8 five to seven

5 R4.17 P Listen and practise the times in 3a) and 4.

6 a) R4.18 Listen and write five times.

b) Work in pairs. Compare answers.

7 a) Look at pictures 1 and 2. Fill in the gaps with these words.

> ~~What~~   time   half   it   to

1 Excuse me. _What_ time is ...., please?
It's twenty .... three.

2 What .... is your English class?
It's at .... past eight.

b) R4.19 P Listen and check. Listen again and practise.

8 Work in new pairs. Student A → p89. Student B → p95.

1 a) R4.20 Look at the pictures. Listen to the sounds and words.

/θ/   /ð/

three

mother

b) P Listen again and practise.

2 a) R4.21 Listen to these words. Notice how we say *th* in these words.

/θ/	three thirteen thirty month think thing thanks birthday Thursday

/ð/	mother father brother this that these those the then they with their

b) P Listen again and practise.

3 a) R4.22 P Listen to these sentences. Listen again and practise.

1 I think that's your mother.
2 Are those your things?
3 It's their brother's birthday on Thursday.
4 I think that man's thirty-three.
5 Thanks for those thirteen emails.
6 This is the first Thursday of the month.

b) Work in pairs. Practise the sentences.

4 Review   Language Summary 4, p106

1 Choose the correct verbs. V4.1

1 (like) / work football
2 study / live English
3 like / work in an office
4 have / study two children
5 work / like rock music
6 live / have in the centre of the city
7 study / live languages
8 have / live in a flat
9 have / work a car
10 work / like for a German company

2 a) Write sentences about you with these words. Use the positive (+) or negative (–) form of *like, have, live, work* or *study*. G4.1

1 coffee   *I don't like coffee.*
2 a mobile   *I have a mobile.*
3 in a small flat
4 Japanese
5 for a British company
6 Chinese food
7 a brother
8 in the capital of my country
9 for a computer company
10 English at a language school

b) Work in pairs. Compare sentences. How many are the same?

3 Match the verbs in A to the words / phrases in B. V4.2

A	B
go to	DVDs
go	concerts
watch	shopping
play	TV
eat	computer games
watch	out
go to	tennis
go	the cinema
play	out with friends

4 a) Make questions about rock stars Mike and Kim Black. G4.2

1 married / Are / Mike and Kim ?   *Are Mike and Kim married?*
2 live / do / Where / they / in the UK?
3 a house / have / they / in the USA / Do ?
4 like / do / music / What / they ?
5 do / in their free time / they / What / do ?
6 go to / Do / concerts / they ?
7 do / What / like / they / food ?
8 the cinema / go to / they / Do ?

b) Work in pairs. Ask and answer the questions in 4a).

5 a) Write the letters in these things you can buy in a shop. V4.3

1 m a p
2 sw _ _ ts
3 b _ tt _ _ ies
4 p _ s _ c _ rd
5 n _ w _ p _ _ er
6 m _ g _ z _ _ e
7 b _ _ th _ ay   c _ _ d
8 ch _ w _ _ g   g _ m
9 t _ ss _ es
10 b _ x of ch _ c _ l _ _ es

b) Work in pairs. Compare answers.

Progress Portfolio

a) Tick (✓) the things you can do in English.

☐ I can talk about things I have and don't have.

☐ I can say where I live and work.

☐ I can talk about things I do in my free time.

☐ I can ask people about their free time.

☐ I can buy things in a shop.

☐ I can say the days of the week.

☐ I can tell the time.

b) What do you need to study again? ● 4A–D

5 Day-to-day life

5A A typical day

> **Vocabulary** daily routines
> **Grammar** Present Simple (*he, she, it*): positive and negative
> **Review** telling the time; Present Simple (*I, you, we, they*); free time activities

QUICK REVIEW ●●●
Write six times (*6.30, 9.10*, etc.). Work in pairs. Take turns to say your times. Write your partner's times. Are they correct?

Daily routines

1 **a)** Look at the pictures of Carol's routine. Then match these words or phrases to pictures 1–10.

> get up *1*   go to bed   leave home
> get home   start work   finish work
> have breakfast   have lunch
> have dinner   sleep

b) R5.1 P Listen and practise.

c) Match the words and phrases in 1a) to these times of day.

morning	*get up*
afternoon	
evening	
night	

2 **a)** Work in pairs. Tell your partner what time you do the things in 1a) in the week. What do you do at the same time?

> I get up at seven o'clock.   I get up at half past six.

b) Tell the class things that you and your partner do at the same time.

> Yoshi and I leave home at eight.

Carol's routine

3 **a)** Check these words with your teacher.

> university   midday   midnight   before (10.30)
> after (10.30)   about (10.30)

b) Look again at pictures 1–10. Then read about Carol's routine on p39 and fill in the gaps with the correct times.

c) R5.2 Listen and check.

Real World **In a restaurant**

4 **a)** Read the conversation. Find all the words for food and drink.

WAITER | CUSTOMERS

WAITER: Are you ready to order?

CUSTOMERS: Yes. Can I have (the chicken salad), please? And can I have (the vegetable lasagne)?

WAITER: Certainly.

WAITER: What would you like to drink?

CUSTOMERS: (A Coke) for me, please. And can we have (a bottle of mineral water)?

WAITER: Still or sparkling?

CUSTOMERS: Sparkling, please.

WAITER: OK. Thanks very much.

WAITER: Would you like a dessert?

CUSTOMERS: Not for me, thanks. (The apple pie) for me. And (two coffees), please.

WAITER: Certainly.

CUSTOMERS: Excuse me. Can we have the bill, please?

WAITER: Of course.

CUSTOMERS: Thanks a lot.

b) Read the conversation again. Find:

1 two questions with *can I have* … .
2 two questions with *can we have* … .
3 two questions with *would you like* … .

RW5.1 p109

Help with Listening **Sentence stress (2)**

5 **R5.10** Look again at **4a)**. Listen again and notice the sentence stress.
Are you ready to order?

6 **a)** **R5.11** **P** Listen and practise the sentences in **4a)**. Copy the stress.

b) Work in groups of three. Practise the conversation in **4a)**. Take turns to be the waiter / waitress.

7 **a)** Work in the same groups. Write a conversation between a waiter / waitress and two customers at the New Moon restaurant. Use language from **4a)** and food and drink from the menu.

b) Practise your conversation until you can remember it.

c) Role-play your conversation for the class. Listen to other groups' conversations. What do they order?

8

9

10

VOCABULARY IN CONTEXT

Vocabulary frequency adverbs and phrases with *every*
Review food and drink (3); Present Simple; time phrases with *on, in, at*

QUICK REVIEW ●●●
Work in pairs. Write all the food and drink on the menu at the New Moon restaurant. Check your list with another pair. Then check on p42.

1 a) Look at these frequency adverbs. Fill in the gaps with *usually* and *not usually*.

always .... sometimes .... never
100% 0%

b) Put these phrases with *every* in order.

every day *1*   every year   every week   every month

c) R5.12 P Listen and practise the words and phrases in 1a) and 1b).

2 a) Check these words with your teacher.

early   late   tired   busy   together

b) R5.13 Read and listen to Pete and Maggie's Sunday routines. What do they always do together on Sundays?

On Sundays I always get up early. I never have breakfast because I play football every Sunday morning. I get home at midday and then I sometimes sleep for an hour or two. I don't usually go out in the afternoon, I usually watch football on TV. And Maggie and I have dinner together at the same restaurant every Sunday evening.

I'm always tired on Sundays because I work every Saturday. I always have breakfast in bed and I never get up before midday! I usually phone my friends in the afternoon, and I sometimes go and see my parents. In the evening Pete and I always have dinner at a restaurant called the New Moon. It isn't usually very busy and the food is fantastic!

Maggie

Pete

3 a) Read about Pete and Maggie again. What does each person always, usually, sometimes, never do on Sundays?

b) Work in pairs. Compare answers.

Help with Vocabulary Frequency adverbs and phrases with *every*

4 Read these rules and the examples.

● Frequency adverbs go after *be*:
I'm always tired on Sundays.
It's not usually very busy.
● Frequency adverbs go before other verbs:
I never have breakfast.
I don't usually go out.
● Phrases with *every* are usually at the end of the sentence:
I work every Saturday.
I play football every Sunday morning.

TIP! ● We can say: *I'm always tired on Sunday / Sundays.*

V5.4 p108

5 a) Make these sentences true for you. Use frequency adverbs or phrases with *every*.

1 I have rice for dinner.
I don't usually have rice for dinner.
2 I eat out at the weekend.
3 I'm tired on Mondays.
4 I'm busy in the week.
5 I go shopping on Saturdays.
6 I get up early at the weekend.
7 I'm late for my English class.

b) Work in pairs. Compare sentences.

6 a) Write two true sentences and two false sentences about your Sunday routine.

b) Work in pairs. Say your sentences. Guess if your partner's sentences are true or false.

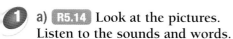

Help with Sounds /w/ and /v/

1 a) R5.14 Look at the pictures. Listen to the sounds and words.

/w/

waiter

/v/

vegetables

b) P Listen again and practise.

2 a) R5.15 Listen to these words. Notice how we say *w* and *v* in these words.

/w/
waiter	always	women	when
work	where	Wednesday
week	weekend	twelve

/v/
vegetables	very	evening
never	live	every	vocabulary
five	seven	eleven

b) P Listen again and practise.

3 a) R5.16 P Listen to the conversation. Listen again and practise.

A Where do you work?
B I'm a waiter and I work in a very nice café in Vienna.
A When do you work?
B I work every evening from five to eleven in the week.
A Do you work at the weekend?
B Yes, I work seven days a week.

b) Work in pairs. Practise the conversation.

5 Review   Language Summary 5, p108

1 a) Read these sentences about a typical day. Complete the verbs. **V5.1**

1 I **g** _et_ up at 7.00 in the week.
2 I **h**............. breakfast at 7.30.
3 I **l**............. home at 8.30.
4 I **s**............. work / school at 9.00.
5 I **h**............. lunch at 1.00.
6 I **f**............. work / school at 5.30.
7 I **g**............. home at 6.00.
8 I **h**............. dinner at 8.00.
9 I **g**............. to bed at midnight.

b) Tick (✓) the sentences in 1a) that are true for you. Make the other sentences true for you.

c) Work in pairs. Compare your daily routines.

2 a) Put the verbs in brackets in the Present Simple. **G5.1**

My best friend's name is Rico and he ¹ _lives_ (live) in London. He ²............. (work) in a hotel, but he ³............. (not like) his job very much. In his free time he ⁴............. (go) to the cinema, ⁵............. (study) English and ⁶............. (watch) football on TV. He's married and he ⁷............. (not have) any children, but his wife ⁸............. (have) four cats!

b) Work in pairs. Compare answers. Check your partner's spelling.

3 a) Make questions about Rico with these words. **G5.2**

1 Where / live / Rico / does ?
   Where does Rico live?
2 work / Where / does / he ?
3 his job / he / Does / like ?
4 do / in his free time / What / he / does ?
5 any children / he / Does / have ?
6 his wife / cats / like / Does ?

b) Work in pairs. Ask and answer the questions. Then check your answers in 2a).

4 Choose the correct words. **V5.2**

1 ⟨on⟩ / at Thursday
2 in / at the morning
3 on / in Thursday morning
4 in / at night
5 on / in the afternoon
6 in / at the weekend
7 in / at the week
8 at / on midday
9 on / in the evening
10 on / in Sunday evening
11 in / at midnight
12 at / on half past six

5 a) Write the words. **RW5.1**

WAITER

1 Are you r _eady_ to o............. ?
2 W............. would you like to d............. ?
3 W............. you l............. a dessert?

CUSTOMER

a) N _ot_ for me, t............. .
b) A Coke f............. me, p............. .
c) Yes. C............. I h............. the lasagne, please?

b) Match questions 1–3 to answers a)–c).

c) Work in pairs. Practise the questions and answers in 5a).

Progress Portfolio

a) Tick (✓) the things you can do in English.

☐ I can talk about my routine and other people's routines.
☐ I can use time phrases.
☐ I can ask people about their routines and free time.
☐ I can understand a simple menu.
☐ I can order food and drink in a restaurant.
☐ I can use frequency adverbs.

b) What do you need to study again? ● 5A–D

6 Towns and cities

Vocabulary places in a town or city (1)
Grammar *a, some, a lot of; there is / there are*: positive
Review frequency adverbs; Present Simple; adjectives (1)

QUICK REVIEW ●●●
Write sentences about things that you: always, usually, sometimes, never do on Saturday. Work in pairs. Tell your partner your sentences:
A *I always get up late on Saturday.* **B** *Me too. / Oh, I usually get up early.*

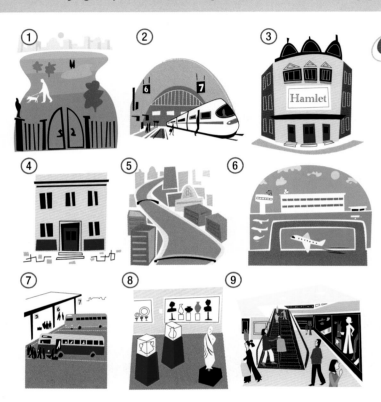

Places in a town or city (1)

1 **a)** Match these words to pictures 1–9.

> a building *4*   a museum   a theatre   a shopping centre
> a park   a river   a station   a bus station   an airport

b) **R6.1** **P** Listen and practise.

My city

2 **a)** Check these words with your teacher.

> famous   great   hot springs   swim   a train   a mile

b) Look at the photos of Bath, a famous city in England. Which things from **1a)** can you see in the photos?

3 **a)** **R6.2** Read and listen to Susan. Does she like living in Bath?

b) Read about Bath again. Tick (✓) the true sentences. Correct the false sentences.

1 Bath is in ~~the USA~~. *England*
2 It's a very beautiful city. ✓
3 Susan goes to the Thermae Bath Spa every Friday.
4 The Jane Austen Centre is a theatre.
5 There are trains to London every 30 minutes.
6 Bath doesn't have an airport.

I live in Bath, a city in England. It's a very beautiful place. There are a lot of old buildings in the centre and there are some very nice parks. Bath is famous for its hot springs, and you can swim in the hot water at the Thermae Bath Spa. I go there every Sunday, it's great! In the centre of Bath there are five theatres and some very good museums, including the Roman Baths and the Jane Austen Centre, about the famous English writer. There are also a lot of good restaurants and hotels, and there's a big new shopping centre called SouthGate. There are trains to London every half an hour, and there's an airport in Bristol, only 15 miles away. I think Bath is a great place to live.

Susan

Help with Grammar *a, some, a lot of;* *there is / there are:* positive

4 **a)** Match sentences 1–3 to pictures A–C.

1 There's **a person** in the park.
2 There are **some people** in the park.
3 There are **a lot of people** in the park.

b) Fill in the gaps with 's (= is) or *are*.

SINGULAR
There _'s_ **a** big new shopping centre.
There _____ **an** airport in Bristol.

PLURAL
There _____ **five** theatres.
There _____ **some** very nice parks.
There _____ **a lot of** old buildings.

G6.1 p111

5 **a)** Look at these sentences about Bath. Fill in the gaps with 's or *are*.

1 There _'s_ a beautiful river.
2 There _____ two cinemas.
3 There _____ a bus station.
4 There _____ some hot springs.
5 There _____ a nice café near the station.
6 There _____ two five-star hotels.
7 There _____ a famous restaurant called Sally Lunn's.
8 There _____ a lot of trains to London every day.

b) R6.3 Listen and check. Notice how we say *there's* and *there are*.

There's /ðeəz/ a beautiful river.
There are /ðeərə/ two cinemas.

c) P Listen again and practise.

6 **a)** Choose the correct words.

1 There's a / some station.
2 There are a / three parks.
3 There are a / some good museums.
4 There's a / some bus station.
5 There are some / a beautiful buildings.
6 There's a / an old theatre.
7 There are an / a lot of very good restaurants.
8 There are some / a nice hotels.

b) Work in pairs. Compare answers. Which sentences are true for the town or city you are in now?

Get ready ... Get it right!

7 Write sentences about a town or city you know (not the town or city you're in now). Use *there is*, *there are* and words from 1a).

In ... there are some beautiful parks.
There are a lot of nice restaurants.
There's a big shopping centre.

8 **a)** Work in pairs. Tell your partner about your town or city in 7.

b) Tell the class two things about your partner's town or city.

Vocabulary places in a town or city (2)
Grammar *there is* / *there are*: negative, *yes* / *no* questions and short answers; *any*
Help with Listening linking (1)
Review *a, some, a lot of*; *there is* / *there are*: positive

QUICK REVIEW ● ● ●
Work in pairs. Say sentences about the town or city you are in now. Use *there is* and *there are*: **A** *There are some good restaurants in the centre.* **B** *Yes, and there's a nice park.*

Places in a town or city (2)

 a) Match these words to pictures 1–9.

> a road *3*   a post office
> a chemist's   a bank
> a market   a supermarket
> a bus stop   a square
> a cashpoint / an ATM

b) R6.4 P Listen and practise.

c) Work in pairs. Test your partner.

(What's picture 3?)

(It's a road.)

Welcome to my home

 a) R6.5 Look at the photo of Susan and her friend, Isabel. Listen to their conversation. Put these things in the order they talk about them.

Susan's flat *1*
restaurants
shops
trains and buses
banks

b) Listen again. Choose the correct words.

1 Susan (likes) / *doesn't like* living in her flat.
2 There are *some* / *a lot of* shops in Susan's road.
3 There's a cashpoint at the *supermarket* / *post office*.
4 It's *a mile* / *two miles* to the centre of Bath.
5 There are buses to the centre of Bath every *ten* / *twenty* minutes.
6 There are some nice restaurants *near Susan's house* / *in the centre*.

c) Work in pairs. Compare answers.

Isabel

Susan

Help with Grammar *there is / there are*: negative, *yes / no* questions and short answers; *any*

3 **a)** Fill in the gaps with *aren't* or *isn't*.

NEGATIVE (–)
1 There _____ a station near here.
2 There _____ any good restaurants near here.

b) Fill in the gaps with *is*, *are*, *isn't* or *aren't*.

YES / NO QUESTIONS (?)	SHORT ANSWERS
Is there a bank?	Yes, there _____ . No, there _____ .
_____ there any shops?	Yes, there are. No, there _____ .

c) Look again at the sentences in **3a)** and **3b)**. Then choose the correct word in this rule.

● We use *some / any* in negatives and questions with *there are*.

G6.2 p111

Help with Listening Linking (1)

4 R6.6 Listen to these sentences. Notice the linking between the **consonant** sounds and the **vowel** sounds.

1 There's an expensive market.
2 There are some old buildings.
3 There isn't an airport.
4 There aren't any museums.
5 Is there a post office?
6 Are there any nice old cafés?

5 R6.7 P Listen and practise the sentences in **4** and the short answers.

There's an expensive market.

6 **a)** Write sentences about places near Susan's flat.

1 (✓) a supermarket
There's a supermarket.
2 (✗) a shopping centre
There isn't a shopping centre.
3 (✓) a market
4 (✗) any museums
5 (✓) a park
6 (✗) a square
7 (✗) any nice cafés
8 (✓) a lot of old houses

b) Work in pairs. Compare answers.

7 Work in the same pairs. Student A → p86. Student B → p92.

Get ready ... Get it right!

8 Look at the picture and the places (a cinema, hotels, etc.) Write eight questions to ask another student about places near his / her home. Use *Is there a ... ?* and *Are there any ... ?*.

Is there a cinema near your home?
Are there any hotels?

a cinema · hotels · shops · a park · a post office · a shopping centre · a supermarket · good restaurants · a station · a market · nice cafés · a bus stop · old buildings

9 **a)** Work in pairs. Ask your questions from **8**. Make notes on your partner's answers. Give more information about places near your home if possible.

Is there a cinema near your home?
Yes, there is. It's five minutes away.

b) Work in new pairs. Talk about places near your first partner's home.

There's a cinema near Gabi's home, but there aren't any hotels.

6C Tourist information

Vocabulary things in your bag (2)
Real World at the tourist information centre
Review places in a town or city; telling the time

QUICK REVIEW ● ● ●
Write all the words you know for places in a town or city (*a museum, a park*, etc.). Work in pairs. Compare lists. Which places are near your school? A *There's a museum near the school.*

Things in your bag (2)

1 a) Look at photo A. Match these words to 1–11.

> a wallet 8   a purse   keys   money   a credit card
> a passport   an ID card   a guide book   a map
> a camera   a laptop

b) R6.8 P Listen and practise.

c) Work in pairs. Which things in **1a)** do you have with you?

> I have some money with me.   Yes, me too.

When is it open?

2 a) Check these words with your teacher.

> a tourist   free   open   closed
> (seven) a.m.   (seven) p.m.   a street

b) Look at photo B. Isabel is at the tourist information centre in Bath. Which things from **1a)** can you see in the photo?

3 a) R6.9 Listen and match conversations 1–3 to a)–c).

a) the Roman Baths Museum
b) a map of the city centre
c) the Thermae Bath Spa

b) Listen again. Choose the correct answers.

1 Isabel wants *a map* / *a guide book*.
2 The maps are *free* / *a pound*.
3 The Roman Baths Museum is open from 9 / 10 a.m. to 5 / 6 p.m.
4 It's *open* / *closed* on Mondays.
5 The Thermae Bath Spa is in *Hot Spa Street* / *Hot Bath Street*.
6 It's about *five* / *fifteen* minutes away.

Real World **At the tourist information centre**

4 Read these conversations. Fill in the gaps with these words.

help   minutes   have   map   much   day   open

TOURIST	ASSISTANT

Good morning.

Hello. Can I ¹ _help_ you?

Yes, please.

Do you ² _____ a (map of the city centre)?

Yes, of course. Here you are.

Thank you. How ³ _____ is it?

It's (a pound).

When is the (Roman Baths Museum) open?

It's ⁴ _____ from (nine) a.m. to (five) p.m.

Is it closed on (Mondays)?

No, it's open every ⁵ _____ .

Where's the (Thermae Bath Spa)?

It's in (Hot Bath Street).

Can you show me on this ⁶ _____ ?

Yes, of course. Here it is.
It's about (five) ⁷ _____ away.

Thank you very much.

RW6.1 p111

5 **a)** R6.10 **P** Listen and practise the sentences in **4**.

Good morning.
Hello. Can I help you?

b) Work in pairs. Practise the conversations in **4**. Take turns to be the tourist.

6 **a)** Cover the conversations in **4**. Then choose the correct words or phrases in these conversations.

A

TOURIST   Good morning.
ASSISTANT   Hello. ¹I Can / (Can I) help you?
T   Yes, please. Do you have a map ²in / of the UK?
A   Yes, of course. ³Here you are / Here are you.
T   Thank you. How much ⁴is it / it is?
A   ⁵Is / It's £4.95.

B

T   Good ⁶afternoon / night. When ⁷is / are the Jane Austen Centre open?
A   It's open ⁸from / to 9.45 a.m. ⁹from / to 5.30 p.m.
T   ¹⁰Is it / Is closed on Mondays?
A   No, it's open every ¹¹day / days.
T   Thanks a lot.

C

A   Hello. Can I ¹²show / help you?
T   Yes, please. ¹³Where's / There's the bus station?
A   It's ¹⁴in / at Manvers Street.
T   Can you show me on this ¹⁵card / map?
A   Yes, of course. ¹⁶Here is it / Here it is. It's about ten minutes away.
T   Thank you very much.

b) R6.11 Listen and check.

c) Work in pairs. Practise the conversations in **6a)**. Take turns to be the tourist.

7 Work in new pairs. Student A → p90. Student B → p96.

6D It's my favourite

QUICK REVIEW ● ● ●

Work in pairs. What things do you both have with you today? **A** *Do you have any money with you?* **B** *Yes, I do.* **A** *Me too.* **B** *Do you have an ID card with you?*

Wayne

Monica

Brad

Lisa

1 **a)** Look at the photos. Match these words to clothes 1–14.

> a suit *3*   a tie   a shirt   a T-shirt   a jumper   a jacket   a coat
> a skirt   a dress   trousers   jeans   shoes   trainers   boots

b) R6.12 P Listen and practise.

c) Work in pairs. Test your partner.

> What's number 1?   It's a shirt.

2 R6.13 P Listen and practise these colours.

black   **white**   **yellow**
brown   **red**   **blue**
grey   **pink**   **green**

3 **a)** Look at the photos for two minutes. Remember the people's names, their clothes and the colours.

b) Work in pairs. Student A, close your book. Student B, ask what colour the people's clothes are. Then change roles.

> What colour are Lisa's shoes?   They're brown.

4 **a)** R6.14 Look again at the photos. Listen and put the people in the order you hear them.

b) Listen again. What does each person never wear?

5 **a)** Which clothes and colours do you: usually wear, sometimes wear, never wear? Write three lists.

b) Work in groups. Compare lists.

Help with Vocabulary *favourite*

6 **a)** Fill in the gaps with *This, These, My, Who* or *What*.

1 .... favourite colour is pink.
2 .... is my favourite jacket.
3 .... are my favourite boots.
4 ....'s your favourite colour?
5 ....'s your favourite actor?

b) R6.15 P Listen and practise.

V6.6 p111

7 Work in pairs. Look at p99.

Help with Sounds /tʃ/ and /dʒ/

1 **a)** `R6.16` Look at the pictures. Listen to the sounds and words.

/tʃ/

cheese

/dʒ/

orange juice

b) `P` Listen again and practise.

2 **a)** `R6.17` Listen to these words. Notice how we say the pink and blue letters.

/tʃ/
cheese   cheap   much   chips
chocolate   chicken   children
picture   sandwich   French

/dʒ/
orange juice   jeans   jumper
jacket   manager   page   job
vegetables   language   Japanese

b) `P` Listen again and practise.

3 **a)** Many English first names start with /dʒ/. Work in pairs. How do we say these names?

♂ male		♀ female	
Jack	John	Jane	Jan
James	Jim	Jessica	Jenny
Jason	Jeremy	Julia	Juliet
Joe	Justin	Joanna	Jill
Geoff	George	Gillian	Gina

b) `R6.18` `P` Listen and check. Listen and practise.

6 Review   Language Summary 6, p110

1 Write the letters. `V6.1`

1 p _a_ _r_ k
2 sho _ pi _ g   c _ nt _ e
3 t _ eat _ e
4 s _ ati _ n
5 r _ ve _
6 a _ rpo _ t
7 b _ ild _ ng
8 b _ s   s _ ati _ n
9 m _ se _ m

2 **a)** Choose the correct words. `G6.1`

1 There 's /(are) a lot of old buildings in Bath.
2 There are *some / a* nice parks.
3 There 's / are four theatres.
4 There are *a / a lot of* good hotels.
5 There 's / are a station.
6 There's *an / some* airport.

b) Work in pairs. Are the sentences true or false? Then check on p46.

3 Write the places in a town or city. `V6.2`

1 dora   r _oad_
2 sub spot   b............... s...............
3 kabn   b...............
4 kemtar   m...............
5 repsukemtar   s...............
6 stop focife   p............... o...............
7 rasque   s...............

4 **a)** Fill in the gaps with *'s, are, isn't* or *aren't*. `G6.1` `G6.2`

Ian lives in Barton, in the UK. There ¹ _are_ some shops in Barton, but there ² .... a supermarket. There ³ .... also a nice park, but there ⁴ .... any old buildings. In Ian's road there's a post office, but there ⁵ .... a bank. There ⁶ .... also two cafés near his house, but there ⁷ .... any restaurants.

b) Fill in the gaps with *Is, Are, a* or *any*. `G6.2`

1 _Are_ there _any_ shops in Barton?
2 .... there .... supermarket?
3 .... there .... nice park?
4 .... there .... old buildings?
5 .... there .... post office in Ian's road?
6 .... there .... bank in Ian's road?
7 .... there .... cafés near Ian's house?
8 .... there .... restaurants near Ian's house?

c) Work in pairs. Ask and answer the questions. Use the correct short answers.

5 **a)** Find 14 words for clothes (→↓). `V6.4`

J	A	C	K	E	T	S	C
E	T	V	O	Q	R	K	O
A	S	U	I	T	A	I	A
N	Z	T	S	H	I	R	T
S	D	B	J	E	N	T	L
T	R	O	U	S	E	R	S
E	E	O	M	X	R	B	H
K	S	T	P	O	S	U	O
G	S	S	E	M	T	I	E
S	H	I	R	T	F	N	S

b) Work in pairs. Compare answers.

c) Which of the clothes in 5a) do you never wear?

Progress Portfolio

a) Tick (✓) the things you can do in English.

☐ I can talk about places in a town or city.
☐ I can ask about other towns or cities.
☐ I can say what is in my bag.
☐ I can ask for information at a tourist information centre.
☐ I can talk about clothes and colours.
☐ I can talk about my favourite things and people.

b) What do you need to study again? `6A–D`

53

7 Love it, like it, hate it!

Vocabulary things you like and don't like; *love, like, hate*
Grammar object pronouns
Review *favourite*; Present Simple; free time activities

QUICK REVIEW ● ● ●
What's your favourite: city, sport, shop, film, book, colour? Work in groups of three. Tell the other students your favourite things. Are any the same?
A *My favourite city is Berlin.* **B** *Me too.* **C** *My favourite city is Prague.*

Things you like and don't like

1 a) Match these words and phrases to pictures 1–9.

> soap operas 7   visiting new places   classical music   flying   dancing
> watching sport on TV   animals   horror films   shopping for clothes

b) **R7.1** **P** Listen and practise.

2 Match these phrases to pictures A–D.

> I like ...   I hate ...   I don't like ...   I love ...

 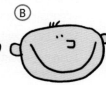 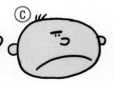 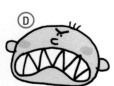

Help with Vocabulary
love, like, hate

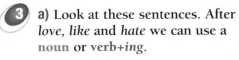

3 a) Look at these sentences. After *love*, *like* and *hate* we can use a **noun** or **verb+ing**.

I love animals.
I like soap operas.
I don't like dancing.
I hate shopping for clothes.

b) Find all the **verb+ing** words in 1a).
    V7.2 p112

4 a) Write three true sentences and three false sentences about things you love, like, don't like and hate. Use words and phrases from 1a).

I don't like horror films.
I love visiting new places.

b) Work in pairs. Say your sentences. Guess if your partner's sentences are true or false.

We're very different

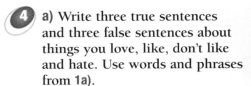

5 a) Check these words with your teacher.

> twins   different   the same   both

b) Do you know any twins? If yes, tell the class about them (names, age, jobs, family, etc.).

> Jenny and I are twins, but our friends tell **us** we're very different. We never go to concerts together because I like rock music and Jenny loves classical music. We both like watching TV, but I love watching sport and Jenny hates it. And Jenny doesn't like horror films, but I love them. But I like having a twin sister. I don't see **her** every week, but she phones **me** every weekend.

Jenny

> Jack's my twin brother, but we don't like the same things. We don't usually eat out together because I like Chinese food and Jack loves Italian food. We both like watching TV, but I love soap operas and he hates **them**. And I don't like flying, but Jack loves **it**. Yes, we're very different, but I like having a twin brother and I always phone **him** at the weekend.

Jack

6 **a)** [R7.2] Read and listen to Jack and Jenny. Find two things they both like.

b) Read about Jack and Jenny again. Fill in the gaps in these sentences with *Jack* or *Jenny*.

1 _Jack_ likes rock music.
2 _____ hates watching sport on TV.
3 _____ doesn't like horror films.
4 _____ loves Italian food.
5 _____ hates soap operas.
6 _____ doesn't like flying.

Help with Grammar Object pronouns

7 **a)** Look at these sentences. Notice the word order.

subject	verb	object
I	love	soap operas.
Jack	hates	them.

b) Look again at the texts about Jack and Jenny. Fill in the table with the object pronouns in blue.

subject pronouns	I	you	he	she	it	we	they
object pronouns		you					

[G7.1] p113

8 **a)** Fill in the gaps with object pronouns.

1 A Do you like dancing?
   B Yes, I love _it_ .
2 A Do you like Madonna?
   B Yes, I like _____ a lot.
3 A Do you like shopping for clothes?
   B No, I hate _____ .
4 A Do you like Johnny Depp?
   B Yes, I love _____ .
5 A Do you like soap operas?
   B No, I hate _____ .
6 A Do you like dogs?
   B Yes, but they don't like _____ !

b) [R7.3] [P] Listen and check. Listen again and practise.

Do you like dåncing?   Yĕs, I lŏve it.

c) Work in pairs. Take turns to ask the questions in 8a). Answer for you.

9 **a)** Write five questions with *Does … like … ?* about Jack and Jenny.

Does Jack like rock music?

b) Work in pairs. Ask and answer the questions.

Get ready … Get it right!

10 Work in new pairs. Student A → p90.
Student B → p96.

55

Can you drive?

Vocabulary abilities
Grammar *can* for ability
Help with Listening *can* or *can't*
Review things you like and don't like; Present Simple questions

QUICK REVIEW ●●●
Work in pairs. Ask questions and find four things you both like:
A *Do you like classical music?* **B** *Yes, I do. / No, I don't.*

Abilities

1 **a)** Match these words and phrases to pictures 1–10.

> swim *4*   cook   drive   sing   ski
> play basketball   play the piano
> play the guitar   speak German   ride a bike

b) R7.4 **P** Listen and practise.

c) Work in pairs. Mime activities from **1a)**. Guess your partner's activities.

I can't swim!

2 Match sentences 1–4 to pictures A–D.

1 Help! I can't swim!
2 She can play the piano.
3 Sorry, we can't speak Chinese.
4 They can ski very well.

你好

Help with Grammar *can*: positive and negative

3 We use *can* or *can't* to talk about ability. Look at these sentences. Then read the rule.

POSITIVE (+)

She	can	play	the piano.
They	can	ski.	

NEGATIVE (−)

I	can't	swim.	
We	can't	speak	Chinese.

● *Can* and *can't* are the same for *I, you, he, she, it, we* and *they.*

TIP! ● We sometimes use *(very) well* with *can*:
They can ski **(very) well**.   **G7.2** p113

Help with Listening *can* or *can't*

4 **a)** R7.5 Listen to these sentences. Notice how we say *can* and *can't*. Is *can* stressed? Is *can't* stressed?

Help! I can't /kɑːnt/ swim!
She can /kən/ play the piano.
Sorry, we can't /kɑːnt/ speak Chinese.
They can /kən/ ski very well.

b) R7.6 Listen to six sentences. Do you hear *can* or *can't*?

5 R7.6 P Listen again and practise.

I can /kən/ play the guitar.

6 **a)** Write three true sentences and three false sentences about you and your family. Use *can* or *can't*.

My sister can speak Russian very well.
I can't ride a bike.

b) Work in pairs. Say your sentences. Guess if your partner's sentences are true or false.

Help with the children

7 **a)** R7.7 Look at the photo. Mrs Jones wants an au pair to help with her children, Ella and Daniel. Listen to the interview. Does Maria get the job?

b) Listen again. Put a tick (✓) for the things Maria can do. Put a cross (✗) for the things she can't do.

1 cook ✓   6 play tennis
2 drive   7 play the piano
3 speak German   8 sing
4 speak French   9 play the guitar
5 swim

c) Work in pairs. Compare answers.

Help with Grammar *can: yes / no* questions and short answers

8 Look at these questions. Then fill in the gaps in the short answers with *can* or *can't*.

YES / NO QUESTIONS (?)	SHORT ANSWERS
Can you cook?	Yes, I ....
Can you play the piano?	No, I ....
Can he play the guitar?	Yes, he ....
Can she speak German?	No, she ....

G7.3 p113

9 R7.8 P Listen and practise the questions and short answers in **8**.

Can /kən/ you cook? Yes, I can /kæn/.

10 Work in pairs. Student A → p91. Student B → p97.

Get ready ... Get it right!

11 Make a list of things you can do.

play the guitar

12 **a)** Work in new pairs. Ask questions to find things you can both do. Use your list from **11**.

(Can you play the guitar?)   (Yes, I can. / No, I can't.)

b) Tell the class things you can both do.

Maria

Mrs Jones

7C # Directions

Vocabulary prepositions of place
Real World asking for and giving directions
Review abilities; *can*; places in a town or city (1) and (2)

QUICK REVIEW ●●●
Work in pairs. Find four things you can do, but your partner can't do: **A** *Can you play the guitar?* **B** *No, I can't.* **A** *Oh, I can!*

Where's the café?

1 a) Write ten places in a town or city.

a restaurant   a café

b) Work in groups. Compare lists. Do you have the same places?

Help with Vocabulary
Prepositions of place

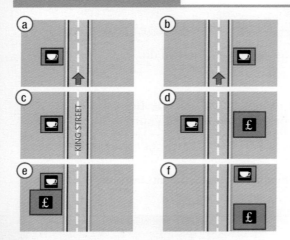

2 Where's the café? Match pictures a)–f) to sentences 1–6.

1 It's **in** King Street. *c)*
2 It's **near** the bank.
3 It's **next to** the bank.
4 It's **opposite** the bank.
5 It's **on** the left.
6 It's **on** the right.

TIP! • We can say **in** King Street or **on** King Street.

V7.4 p112

3 a) R7.9 P Listen and practise the sentences in **2**.

b) Work in pairs. Ask where the café is in pictures a)–f).

> Where's the café in picture c)?

> It's in King Street.

It's over there

4 **a)** Work in new pairs. Maria now lives with the Jones family in Hampton. Look at the map on p59. What are places 1–12?

b) Work in the same pairs. Say where a place is on the map. Your partner guesses the place.

> It's in New Road, opposite the park.

> The cinema.

5 **a)** Look at the photo of Maria. She's is at ✳ on the map. Read conversations A–C. Fill in the gaps with the correct places.

A
MARIA   Excuse me. Where's the ¹ *post office* ?
MAN   It's over there, near the cinema.
MARIA   Oh, yes. I can see it. Thanks.
MAN   You're welcome.

B
MARIA   Excuse me. Where's the ² _____ ?
MAN   Go along this road and turn left. That's Park Street. The ³ _____ is on the right, next to the theatre.
MARIA   Thank you very much.
MAN   You're welcome.

C
MARIA   Excuse me. Is there a ⁴ _____ near here?
WOMAN   Yes, there is. Go along this road and turn right. The ⁵ _____ is on the left, opposite the station.
MARIA   OK, thanks a lot.

b) R7.10 Listen and check.

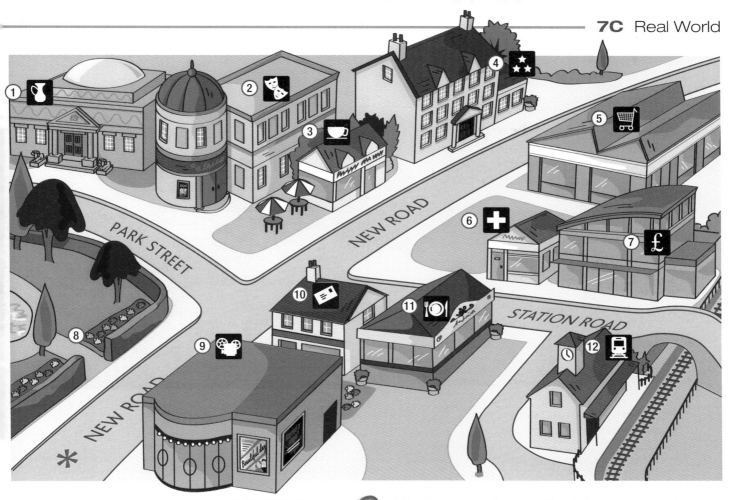

Real World Asking for and giving directions

6 Fill in the gaps with these words.

| ~~Excuse~~ | to | turn | on | road | here | over |

ASKING FOR DIRECTIONS
¹*Excuse* me. Where's the (museum)?
Excuse me. Is there a (bank) near ² _____ ?

GIVING DIRECTIONS
Go along this ³ _____ and turn left.
Go along this road and ⁴ _____ right.
That's (Park Street).
The (museum) is on the right, next ⁵ _____
   the (theatre).
The (bank) is ⁶ _____ the left, opposite
   the (station).
It's ⁷ _____ there, near the (cinema).

RW7.1 p113

7 a) **R7.11** **P** Listen and practise the sentences
in **6**.

Excuse me. Where's the museum?

b) Work in pairs. Practise the conversations
in **5a)**. Take turns to be Maria.

8 a) Look again at the map. Read these conversations.
Choose the correct words.

1

A Excuse ¹*you* / *me*. Is there a restaurant near ²*here* / *there*?
B Yes, there is. Go along this road and turn ³*left* / *right*.
   That's Station Road. The restaurant is ⁴*in* / *on* the right,
   ⁵*near* / *in* the station.
A Thank you very much.

2

A Excuse me. ⁶*Where's* / *What's* the theatre?
B It's ⁷*near* / *over* there, ⁸*opposite* / *next to* the museum.
A Oh yes. I can see it. Thanks a lot.
B You're welcome.

3

A Excuse me. Is there a supermarket ⁹*next to* / *near* here?
B Yes, there is. Go ¹⁰*to* / *along* this road. The supermarket
   is on the ¹¹*left* / *right*, opposite the ¹²*hotel* / *café*.
A Thanks a lot.

b) **R7.12** Listen and check.

c) Work in pairs. Practise the conversations in **8a)**.
Take turns to ask for directions.

9 Work in new pairs. You are at ✳ on the map. Ask for
directions to places on the map. Are your partner's
directions correct?

Vocabulary things people do online
Review *there is / there are*; *can*;
Present Simple questions

VOCABULARY IN CONTEXT

QUICK REVIEW ● ● ●
Write sentences with *there is / there are* about
places near your school. Work in pairs. Compare
sentences. Do you know your partner's places?
A *There's a nice café in New Street, opposite the
cinema.* **B** *Really? What's it called?*

1 **a)** Look at the questionnaire. Fill in the
gaps in phrases 1–8 with these words.

> send sell watch listen music
> theatre friends holidays

TIPS! • We say *receive emails* or *get emails*.
• *online* = connected to the Internet

b) R7.13 **P** Listen and practise.

2 Work in pairs. What can people do at
these websites?

> You can download music at emusic.com.

3 **a)** Work in new pairs. What other things
can people do online? Make a list.
listen to music book a hotel

b) Compare lists with another pair.
Do you have the same things?

4 **a)** R7.14 Look at the photo. Listen to
Alice's interview. Put a tick (✓) or a cross
(✗) in column B of the questionnaire.

b) Listen again. Answer these questions.

1 Does Alice get a lot of emails every day?
2 What's her favourite website?
3 Where does her sister live?
4 What does she buy on Amazon?
5 Is she married?
6 Does she have an iPod?

Alice

Internet questionnaire

A	B	C
things people do online	**Alice (✓ or ✗)**	**your partner (✓ or ✗)**
1 _send_ and receive emails		
2 buy concert or _____ tickets		
3 _____ videos or TV programmes		
4 _____ to the radio		
5 chat to _____ or family		
6 buy and _____ things		
7 book flights or _____		
8 download _____		

5 **a)** Work in pairs. Look again at the questionnaire. Interview
your partner. Put a tick (✓) or a cross (✗) in column C.
Give more information if possible.

> Do you send and
> receive emails?

> Yes, I do. I get about
> 50 emails a day!

> Do you buy concert or
> theatre tickets online?

> No, I don't.

b) Work in new pairs. Talk about your partner in **5a**).

c) Tell the class two things about your first partner.

Help with Sounds /s/ and /ʃ/

1 a) R7.15 Look at the pictures. Listen to the sounds and words.

/s/

suit

/ʃ/

shirt

b) P Listen again and practise.

2 a) R7.16 Listen to these words. Notice how we say the pink and blue consonants.

/s/	suit small skirt sell centre city police pencil expensive lesson Spanish

/ʃ/	shirt she shop sugar tissues sure Turkish British Egyptian Russian Spanish

b) P Listen again and practise.

3 a) R7.17 P Listen to this poem. Listen again and practise.

Sharon Smith has a small shop
In Shanghai city centre
She sells Spanish skirts
And Turkish shirts
And expensive British suits
She sells Egyptian boots
And Russian coats
What can she sell you?

b) Work in pairs. Take turns to say lines of the poem.

7 Review

Language Summary 7, p112

1 a) Write the letters. V7.1

1 soa _p_ o _p_ era _s_
2 ani _ a _ s
3 ho _ _ or fil _ s
4 da _ ci _ g
5 f _ yin _
6 cla _ _ ical mu _ ic
7 wa _ c _ ing spo _ t on T _
8 vi _ itin _ ne _ pla _ es
9 s _ o _ ping for clo _ _ es

b) Tick (✓) three things you like. Then find two students who like the same things.

2 Fill in the gaps with these verbs. V7.2

~~like~~ likes love loves
hate hates don't like
doesn't like

1 I _like_ watching football.
2 I .... playing tennis.
3 Harry .... rice.
4 He .... vegetables.
5 Jane .... watching TV.
6 We .... soap operas.
7 She .... coffee.
8 We .... learning English.

3 Choose the correct words. G7.1

1 Where are (they) / them?
2 She / Her doesn't know we / us.
3 Does he / him like I / me?
4 I / me know she / her.
5 We / Us never see they / them.
6 Do you live with he / him?

4 a) Look at the pictures. Write three true sentences and three false sentences about you. Use _can_ and _can't_. V7.3 G7.2

¡HOLA!

I can play the guitar well.
I can't speak Spanish.

b) Work in pairs. Say your sentences. Guess if your partner's sentences are true or false.

5 a) Cross out the wrong words. V7.5

1 send / get / ~~buy~~ emails
2 download _music / videos / friends_
3 buy _concert / theatre / radio_ tickets
4 watch _TV programmes / videos / the radio_
5 book _flights / friends / holidays_
6 chat to _friends / family / emails_
7 listen to _music / the radio / flights_
8 _buy / chat / sell_ things online

b) Work in pairs. Compare answers. Which things in **5a)** do you do online?

Progress Portfolio

a) Tick (✓) the things you can do in English.

☐ I can talk about things I like and don't like.

☐ I can ask about things other people like and don't like.

☐ I can say things I can and can't do.

☐ I can ask what other people can do.

☐ I can ask for, give and understand simple directions.

☐ I can talk about things I do online.

b) What do you need to study again? ● 7A–D

8 Days to remember

Vocabulary adjectives (2)
Grammar Past Simple of *be*: positive and negative
Review adjectives (1); *favourite*

QUICK REVIEW ●●●

Write the opposites of these adjectives: *good, hot, big, new, cheap, beautiful*. Work in pairs. Compare answers. Then say one sentence for each adjective: **A** *I have a new computer.* **B** *My computer is very old.*

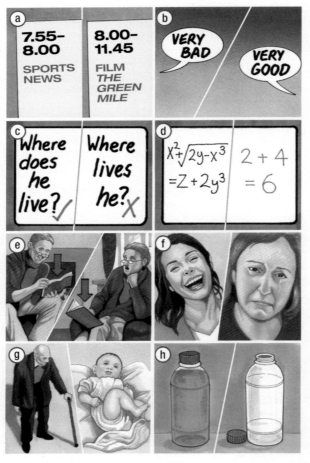

Three amazing days

2 **a)** Check these words with your teacher.

> a stadium   a seat   New Year's Eve
> fireworks   a party   a match

b) **R8.2** Read and listen to Melanie, Tania and Pascal. What were their 'amazing days'?

c) Read the texts again. Choose the correct words in these sentences.

1 The Beatles' last concert was in *the UK* / (*the USA*).
2 The concert was about *an hour* / *half an hour* long.
3 Tania was in Sydney with her *parents* / *friends*.
4 The fireworks at midnight were *fantastic* / *boring*.
5 Pascal's friends were from *France* / *Brazil*.
6 He was at the match with *two* / *three* other people.

> I was at the Beatles' last concert. It was in San Francisco in 1966. There were 25,000 people at the concert, but the stadium wasn't full – there were about 17,000 empty seats! The concert wasn't very long, only 33 minutes, but I was very happy to be there. I was only sixteen at the time.

Adjectives (2)

1 **a)** Match these adjectives to pictures a)–h).

1   short   [a] long
2   happy   ☐ unhappy
3   interesting   ☐ boring
4   full   ☐ empty
5   difficult   ☐ easy
6   right   ☐ wrong
7   old   ☐ young
8   terrible, awful   ☐ great, fantastic, amazing

b) **R8.1** **P** Listen and practise.

Melanie

Help with Grammar Past Simple of *be*: positive and negative

3 **a)** Look at these sentences. Are they in the present or the past?

I **was** at the World Cup Final.
We **were** near the Opera House.
The stadium **wasn't** full.
They **weren't** very happy.

b) Look at the sentences in 3a) again. Then fill in the gaps in the table with *was, wasn't, were* and *weren't*.

POSITIVE (+)	NEGATIVE (−)
I	I **wasn't** (= was not)
you **were**	you **weren't** (= were not)
he / she / it **was**	he / she / it ....
we	we **weren't**
they **were**	they ....

TIP! • The past of *there is / there are* is *there was / there were*.

G8.1 p115

4 **R8.3** **P** Listen and practise. Notice how we say *was* and *were*.

I was /wəz/ *at the World Cup Final.*
We were /wə/ *near the Opera House.*

5 **a)** Choose the correct words.

1 I (was) / were only ten years old.
2 My sisters *wasn't / weren't* at the concert.
3 There *was / were* a lot of people in Sydney that night.
4 John Lennon *was / were* a great musician.
5 The fireworks *was / were* on TV in a lot of countries.
6 I *was / were* very happy after the match.
7 There *wasn't / weren't* any empty seats in the stadium.
8 At 3 a.m. my parents *was / were* very tired, but I *wasn't / weren't*.
9 The concert *wasn't / weren't* expensive – my ticket *was / were* only $4.50!

b) Work in pairs. Compare answers. Who says each sentence: Melanie, Tania or Pascal?

Get ready ... Get it right!

6 Work in groups of three. Look at p99.

I was in Sydney on New Year's Eve 1999. I was only twelve, and I was there with my mum and dad. We were near the Opera House all evening, and at midnight there were some amazing fireworks. Then there was a big party in the city all night. It was a fantastic New Year!

Tania

I was at the World Cup Final in Paris in 1998. I was very young at the time. There were 80,000 people in the stadium, and I was there with two Brazilian friends and their dad. They weren't very happy because it was France 3 Brazil 0, but I was! It was a great match – and I was there!

Pascal

63

8B Happy anniversary!

Vocabulary years and past time phrases
Grammar Past Simple of *be*: questions and short answers; *was born / were born*
Review adjectives; Past Simple of *be*: positive and negative

QUICK REVIEW ● ● ●
Write six adjectives and their opposites (*difficult, easy*, etc.). Work in pairs. Take turns to say an adjective. Your partner says the opposite adjective and a sentence with this adjective: **A** *difficult.* **B** *easy. English is very easy!*

Years and past time phrases

 a) Match 1–6 to a)–f).

1	1887	a)	nineteen eighty
2	1900	b)	twenty ten
3	1980	c)	eighteen eighty-seven
4	2000	d)	two thousand and nine
5	2009	e)	nineteen hundred
6	2010	f)	two thousand

TIP! • We use *in* with years: *in* 1980, etc.

b) R8.4 P Listen and practise.

c) Work in pairs. Say these years.

2012	1977	2018	1815	1990	2003

a) Match pictures A–D to sentences 1–4.

1 Joe was in Paris **last** week. *A*
2 He's at work **now**.
3 He was in bed four hours **ago**.
4 He was at home **yesterday** afternoon.

b) R8.5 P Listen and practise sentences 1–4.

 Fill in the gaps with *yesterday, in, last* or *ago*.

1 I was in a café two hours *ago* .
2 I was at home _____ night.
3 I wasn't in this country _____ 1999.
4 I wasn't at work _____ morning.
5 I was in this class _____ month.
6 I wasn't in this class three months _____ .

An Indian wedding

 a) Check these words with your teacher.

a wedding a bride a groom a wedding anniversary

b) Look at the photos of an Indian wedding. Who is the bride? Who is the groom?

c) R8.6 Listen to Rajeet talk to a friend about his wedding anniversary. Choose the correct words in these sentences.

1 Rajeet and Gita's wedding anniversary is on ⟨Saturday⟩ / Sunday.
2 Their wedding was *two / ten* years ago.
3 Their wedding was in *England / India*.
4 Rajeet's parents *were / weren't* at the wedding.
5 There *was / wasn't* a party after the wedding.

d) Listen again. Answer these questions.

1 Where was the wedding? *In Mumbai.*
2 How old were Rajeet and Gita?
3 How many people were at the wedding?
4 Where was Rajeet's brother?
5 Were Rajeet's sisters at the wedding?
6 How many days was the party?

Help with Grammar Past Simple of *be*: questions and short answers; *was born / were born*

5 WH- QUESTIONS (?)

a) Look at these questions. Notice the word order.

Where	**was**	the wedding?
How old	**were**	Rajeet and Gita?

b) Write these questions in the table.

1 How many people **were** at the wedding?
2 Where **was** Rajeet's brother?

c) Fill in the gaps with *was, were, wasn't* or *weren't*.

YES / NO QUESTIONS (?)	SHORT ANSWERS
.... I / he / she / it at the wedding?	Yes, I / he / she / it was. No, I / he / she / it ....
Were you / we / they at the wedding?	Yes, you / we / they .... No, you / we / they ....

WAS BORN / WERE BORN

d) Fill in the gaps with *was* or *were*.

1 A Where *was* Gita born?
   B She .... born in the UK.

2 A When .... you born?
   B I .... born in 1987.

G8.2 p115

6 R8.7 P Listen and practise the questions and answers in 5.

Where was the wedding?
How old were Rajeet and Gita?

7 a) Choose the correct words.

1 Who *was* / (were) the bride and groom?
2 *Was* / *Were* they the same age?
3 When *was* / *were* the wedding?
4 *Was* / *Were* Rajeet's parents at the wedding?
5 Who *was* / *were* in Australia?
6 Where *was* / *were* Gita born?

b) Work in pairs. Ask and answer the questions.

8 a) Make questions with these words.

1 you / at home / last Sunday / Were ?
   Were you at home last Sunday?
2 you / yesterday evening / were / Where ?
3 three months ago / you / Were / on holiday ?
4 on New Year's Eve 1999 / you / were / Where ?
5 at work / Were / last Monday / you ?
6 you / were / Where / born ?

b) Work in pairs. Ask and answer the questions.

9 a) Write the names of three people you know. Think when and where they were born. Don't write this information.

b) Work in pairs. Ask about the people on your partner's paper.

Who's Mehmet?

He's my brother.

When was he born?

In 1984.

Where was he born?

In Dubai.

Get ready ...
Get it right!

10 Work in new pairs. Student A → p88. Student B → p94.

8C When's your birthday?

QUICK REVIEW ●●●

Work in pairs. Ask your partner where he / she was: three hours ago, yesterday afternoon, at 9 p.m. last Saturday, at 11 a.m. last Sunday, on New Year's Eve last year. **A** *Where were you three hours ago?* **B** *I was at work.*

> **Vocabulary** months and dates
> **Real World** talking about days and dates; making suggestions
> **Help with Listening** linking (2)
> **Review** Past Simple of *be*; past time phrases

Months and dates

1 **a)** R8.8 P Listen and practise the months.

January	May	September
February	June	October
March	July	November
April	August	December

b) Work in pairs. Say a month. Your partner says the next two months.

> June

> July, August

2 **a)** R8.9 P Listen and practise these dates. Notice the letters in **pink**.

1st first	6th sixth	11th eleventh
2nd second	7th seventh	12th twelfth
3rd third	8th eighth	20th twentieth
4th fourth	9th ninth	21st twenty-first
5th fifth	10th tenth	30th thirtieth

b) Work in pairs. Say these dates.

13th	14th	15th	16th	17th	18th	19th	22nd
23rd	24th	25th	26th	27th	28th	29th	31st

c) R8.10 P Listen and check. Listen again and practise.

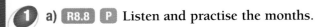

Real World Talking about days and dates

3 Read these questions and answers. Notice the words in **bold**.

1 A What day is it today?
  B (It's) Monday.
2 A What's the date today?
  B (It's) March **the** seventh.
3 A When's your birthday?
  B (It's **on**) June **the** second.

RW8.1 p115

4 R8.11 P Listen and practise the questions and answers in **3**.

5 R8.12 Listen to four conversations. Which dates do you hear?

1 June *20th / 22nd*
2 March *13th / 30th*
3 October *3rd / 23rd*
4 April *1st / 4th*

6 **a)** Write five dates (*March 3rd, August 25th*, etc.).

b) Work in pairs. Say the dates. Write your partner's dates. Check your partner's paper. Are they correct?

c) Ask other students when their birthdays are. Do any students have birthdays in the same month as you?

> When's your birthday, Adela?

> It's on May 25th.

> My birthday's on May 22nd.

Happy birthday!

7 **a)** Check these words with your teacher.

> a present   a play   meet   decide

b) R8.13 Look at the photo. It's Helen's birthday today. Listen to her conversation with her husband, Sam. What do they decide to do this evening?

8 [R8.13] Listen again. Choose the correct words.

1 Helen's present is a *skirt* / (*dress*) .
2 Antonio's is the name of a *shop* / *restaurant*.
3 Helen and Sam go to the cinema every *week* / *month*.
4 The theatre is near the *cinema* / *museum*.
5 They decide to meet at *a café* / *the theatre* at about *6.00* / *7.00*.

Help with Listening Linking (2)

9 **a)** Look at these sentences from Helen and Sam's conversation. Why do we link the words in **pink** and **blue**?

Do you have any good ideas?
We were there a week ago.
See you this evening.

b) [R8.13] Look at R8.13, p124. Listen again and notice the consonant-vowel linking.

Real World Making suggestions

10 Read these sentences. Fill in the gaps with these words.

~~do~~   meet   idea   seven   don't   time

What shall we ¹_do_ (this evening)?

Why don't we (go to the cinema)?
Let's (go to the theatre).

✓ Yes, that's a good ²_____ .
✓✗ Maybe.
✗ No, I ³_____ think so.

Where shall we ⁴_____ ?

Let's meet at (the theatre).

What ⁵_____ shall we meet?

About ⁶_____ o'clock.

[RW8.2] p115

11 [R8.14] [P] Listen and practise the sentences in 10.
What shall we do this evening?

12 **a)** Put this conversation in order.

GEORGE
a) What shall we do tomorrow evening, Jessica? *1*
b) Great! See you there!
c) No, I don't think so.
d) OK. What time shall we meet?
e) Yes, that's a good idea. Where shall we meet?

JESSICA
f) Let's meet at the restaurant.
g) Why don't we go to the cinema? *2*
h) About quarter to eight.
i) OK. Let's go to that Indian restaurant in Old Street.

b) [R8.15] Listen and check.

c) Work in pairs. Practise the conversation in 12a).

13 **a)** Work in new pairs. Write a conversation about next Saturday. Use sentences in **10** and your own ideas.

b) Practise your conversation until you can remember it.

c) Work in groups of four. Role-play your conversations. What do the other pair decide to do on Saturday?

d) Role-play one of your group's conversations for the class.

Sam
Helen

VOCABULARY IN CONTEXT

Vocabulary big numbers
Review making suggestions; months and dates; *was* and *were*

QUICK REVIEW ●●●
Work in pairs. You want to go out together tomorrow evening. Make suggestions about what to do. Decide a place and time to meet. **A** *What shall we do tomorrow evening?* **B** *Why don't we … ?*

1 **a)** Match the numbers in A to the phrases in B.

A	B
150	a thousand
390	a million
1,000	sixteen thousand, two hundred
16,200	a hundred and fifty
750,000	fifty million
1,000,000	three hundred and ninety
50,000,000	seven hundred and fifty thousand

TIP! • We don't use a plural *-s* with *hundred, thousand* or *million*: *three hundred* not ~~three hundreds~~, etc.

b) **R8.16** **P** Listen and practise.

2 **a)** **R8.17** Listen and write the numbers.

b) Work in pairs. Compare answers.

3 **a)** Work on your own. Write five big numbers.

b) Work in new pairs. Say your numbers. Write your partner's numbers. Are they correct?

4 **a)** Check these words with your teacher.

a fêstival   trável   throw   a kïlo   gãrlic

b) Read the article. Fill in the gaps with these numbers.

177,500	70,000,000	1,500
125,000	30,000	150,000

c) **R8.18** Listen to the article and check your answers.

5 **a)** Read the article again. Answer these questions.

1 When and where is La Tomatina?
2 What do people do at this festival?
3 When is the Gilroy Garlic Festival?
4 What food do people eat at this festival?
5 When was the first Glastonbury Festival?
6 When is the next Kumbh Mela?

b) Which two festivals would you like to go to?

Fantastic festivals

There are a lot of fantastic festivals around the world. On the last Wednesday in August, **a)** _____ people travel to Buñol, in Spain, for La Tomatina. At this festival people throw tomatoes at each other – **b)** _____ kilos of them! And for three days every July **c)** _____ people go to the town of Gilroy, in California, for the Gilroy Garlic Festival. Here you can eat garlic bread, garlic chicken, garlic chocolate – and garlic ice cream!

Of course, not all festivals are about food. The UK's favourite music festival is the Glastonbury Festival. Only **d)** _____ people were at the first Glastonbury Festival in June 1970, but in 2008 there were **e)** _____ people there. And for a really *big* festival, there's the amazing Kumbh Mela in India. There's only one Kumbh Mela every 12 years. The festival in 2003 went on for 41 days and **f)** _____ people were there!

The Kumbh Mela, India

1 a) **R8.19** Look at the pictures. Listen to the sounds and words.

/ɔː/

/ɜː/

forty

burger

b) **P** Listen again and practise.

2 a) **R8.20** Listen to these words. Notice how we say the pink and blue letters.

/ɔː/ forty four sport boring awful August daughter small always morning water short

/ɜː/ burger first work shirt skirt Turkish German girl early thirty third surname

b) **P** Listen again and practise.

3 a) **R8.21** **P** Listen to these sentences. Listen again and practise.

1 It's the thirty-first of August.
2 It was a boring morning at work.
3 This small burger is awful.
4 The Turkish girl is always early.
5 It's a German sports company.
6 My daughter has forty-four skirts and thirty-three shirts!

b) Work in pairs. Practise the sentences.

8 Review   Language Summary 8, p114

1 a) Find nine adjectives (→ ↓). **V8.1**

Y	O	U	N	G	A	F	B
M	E	B	S	A	Q	U	O
W	R	O	N	G	K	L	N
T	E	R	R	I	B	L	E
V	E	I	Z	N	I	X	A
L	O	N	G	L	W	I	S
K	U	G	R	E	A	T	Y
H	A	P	P	Y	U	P	A

b) Write the opposites of the adjectives in **1a)**.

young → old

2 Choose the correct words. **G8.1**

1 My dad (was) / were a doctor.
2 These shoes wasn't / weren't expensive, they was / were only £20.
3 I wasn't / weren't at home on Sunday, I was / were at work.
4 My grandparents was / were from Italy.
5 It wasn't / weren't a very good film.
6 I'm sorry we wasn't / weren't at your party. We was / were in France.

3 a) Write six years. **V8.2**

2018   1977

b) Work in pairs. Say your years. Write your partner's years. Are they correct?

4 a) Fill in the gaps with last, yesterday, in or ago. **V8.2**

Luke was …

a) at work an hour _ago_ .
b) in New York _____ week.
c) at a party _____ evening.
d) in Rome _____ Saturday.
e) at university _____ 2003.
f) in India a month _____ .

b) Work in pairs. Put sentences a)–f) in order.

5 a) Make questions with these words. **G8.2**

1 born / Where / you / were ?
   Where were you born?
2 last year / in this country / you / Were ?
3 was / born / your father / Where ?
4 two months ago / Were / in this class / you ?
5 were / on your last birthday / Where / you ?
6 was / English class / When / your first ?

b) Work in pairs. Ask and answer the questions.

6 a) Fill in the gaps with these words. **RW8.2**

What	Why	Where	good
think	meet	let's	shall	past

A ¹ _What_ shall we do on Sunday?
B ² _____ don't we play tennis?
A No, I don't ³ _____ so.
B OK, ⁴ _____ go to the park.
A Yes, that's a ⁵ _____ idea.
   ⁶ _____ shall we meet?
B Let's ⁷ _____ at the station.
A What time ⁸ _____ we meet?
B About half ⁹ _____ two.

b) Work in pairs. Practise the conversation.

Progress Portfolio

a) Tick (✓) the things you can do in English.

☐ I can make sentences and ask questions with was and were.

☐ I can say and understand years and past time phrases.

☐ I can say and understand months and dates.

☐ I can ask about days and dates.

☐ I can make and respond to suggestions.

☐ I can say and understand big numbers.

b) What do you need to study again? ● **8A–D**

9 Going away

Vocabulary transport
Grammar Past Simple: positive (regular and irregular verbs)
Help with Listening Present Simple or Past Simple
Review years, months and dates

QUICK REVIEW ● ● ●
Write the names of four people in your family. Work in pairs. Swap papers. Ask questions about the people and when they were born: **A** *Who's Natalia?* **B** *She's my sister.* **A** *When was she born?* **B** *On June 2nd 1994.*

Transport

1 a) Tick (✓) the words you know. Then check new words in Language Summary 9 **V9.1** p116.

> a car   a bus   a train   a taxi   a bike
> a motorbike   a plane   a boat

b) **R9.1** **P** Listen and practise.

c) <u>Underline</u> the verbs in these sentences.

1 I usually go to work by car.
2 I come to this school by bus.
3 I never travel by plane.
4 I always walk to work.

TIP! ● We say **by** *car,* **by** *bus,* etc.

2 a) Write sentences about you.

1 I … to work / school / university …
   I go to work by bike.
2 I usually … to this school …
3 When I go shopping, I usually …
4 I love travelling …
5 I don't like travelling …
6 I never travel …

b) Work in pairs. Say your sentences. Are any the same?

Bangkok to Brighton

3 a) Check these words with your teacher.

> a tuk-tuk   Thailand   a journey
> raise money for charity

b) Look at the photo. What is the article about, do you think?

c) Read the article. Are your guesses in **3b)** correct?

Let's go by tuk-tuk!

In 2006 two English women, Jo Huxster and Antonia Bolingbroke-Kent, travelled from Thailand to the UK – in a pink tuk-tuk! Jo **had** the idea in 2002 when she **went** to Bangkok on holiday. When she **came** back to England, she **told** her friend Antonia what she **wanted** to do. Antonia **liked** the idea, so in 2006 they went back to Bangkok and **bought** a tuk-tuk called Ting Tong.

Jo and Antonia **started** their journey on May 28th 2006. They travelled for 12 hours every day, usually on very bad roads. All the people they **met** were very friendly and they sometimes **gave** Jo and Antonia food and money. The two women travelled 12,500 miles and **visited** 12 countries. They **arrived** in Brighton, England, 98 days after they **left** Bangkok. After they **got** home, they **wrote** a book called *Tuk-Tuk to the Road*. They also raised £50,000 for charity.

4 Read the article again. Complete the table with the correct dates, places and numbers.

a)	travelled by	tuk-tuk
b)	date started	
c)	place started	
d)	place finished	
e)	miles travelled	
f)	countries visited	12
g)	days travelled	
h)	money raised	

Help with Grammar Past Simple: positive (regular and irregular verbs)

5 REGULAR VERBS

a) Look at the regular Past Simple forms in blue in the article. Then complete these rules with *-d* or *-ed*.

• To make the Past Simple of regular verbs, we usually add .... to the verb.

• For regular verbs that end in *-e* (like, arrive, etc.), we add .... to the verb.

TIP! • The Past Simple of *travel* is *travel**led***.

IRREGULAR VERBS

b) Look at the irregular Past Simple forms in pink in the article. Match them to verbs 1–10.

1 buy *bought*		6	have
2 come		7	leave
3 get		8	meet
4 give		9	tell
5 go		10	write

TIP! • The Past Simple of regular and irregular verbs is the same for *I, you, he, she, it, we* and *they*.

c) Check in Language Summary 9 G9.1 p117. Learn the other irregular verbs in the list.

6 **a)** Write the Past Simple forms of these regular verbs.

1 visit *visited*		7	live
2 watch		8	want
3 play		9	love
4 hate		10	talk
5 walk		11	start
6 work		12	finish

b) R9.2 P Listen and practise. Which Past Simple forms end in /ɪd/?

c) R9.3 P Listen and practise the irregular Past Simple forms in **5b)**.

Help with Listening
Present Simple or Past Simple

7 **a)** R9.4 Listen to these sentences. Notice the difference between the **Present Simple** and the **Past Simple**.

1 I **live** in London. I **lived** in London.
2 We **work** at home. We **worked** at home.
3 They **love** it. They **loved** it.

b) R9.5 Listen to six pairs of sentences. Which do you hear <u>first</u>, the Present Simple or the Past Simple?

1 Past Simple

Around the world by bike

8 **a)** Read about Mark Beaumont's journey. Fill in the gaps with the Past Simple of the verbs in brackets.

b) Work in pairs. Compare answers.

Mark Beaumont, from Scotland, ¹*cycled* (cycle) around the world in only 194 days and 17 hours. Mark ² .... (have) the idea after he ³ .... (leave) Glasgow University in 2007, and he ⁴ .... (start) his journey in Paris on August 5ᵗʰ the same year. He ⁵ .... (travel) 18,300 miles and ⁶ .... (visit) 20 countries, and he ⁷ .... (meet) a lot of interesting people. He also ⁸ .... (write) an online diary and ⁹ .... (get) emails from friends and family every week. He ¹⁰ .... (finish) his journey in Paris on February 15ᵗʰ 2008. His family ¹¹ .... (go) to Paris for the big day, and his mother ¹² .... (tell) the newspapers she ¹³ .... (be) very proud of her son. Mark ¹⁴ .... (raise) over £10,000 for charity.

Get ready … Get it right!

9 Work in groups of three. Look at p99.

9B My last holiday

Vocabulary holiday activities
Grammar Past Simple: negative, questions and short answers
Review Past Simple: positive; frequency adverbs

QUICK REVIEW ● ● ●

Write five regular or irregular verbs and their Past Simple forms. Work in pairs. Say the verbs. Your partner says a sentence with the Past Simple form: **A** *go.* **B** *I went out with friends last night.*

Holiday activities

 a) Tick (✓) the phrases you know. Then do the exercise in **V9.2** p116.

> go on holiday   take photos   go to the beach
> stay with friends or family   stay in a hotel
> go sightseeing   go swimming   go for a walk
> rent a car   travel around   have a good time

b) **R9.6** **P** Listen and practise.

c) What are the Past Simple forms of the verbs in **1a)**?

go → went   take → took

 a) Write four sentences about things you do on holiday. Use *always, usually, sometimes* and phrases from **1a)**.

I always go to the beach.
I usually stay with friends.

b) Work in pairs. Say your sentences. Are any of your partner's sentences true for you?

Favourite places

 a) Check these words with your teacher.

> the sea   an island   the scenery

b) **R9.7** Read and listen to Nancy, Jeff and Bob. Match the people to the photos. Which countries are the places in?

c) Read the texts again. Fill in the gaps in these sentences with *Nancy, Jeff, Bob* or *Liz.*

1 *Nancy* and _____ went on holiday last year.
2 _____ stayed with friends.
3 _____ visited an island.
4 _____ and _____ went for a walk every day.
5 _____ only went to one city.
6 _____ , _____ and _____ stayed in hotels.

Nancy

I went on holiday to Istanbul last year. I didn't stay in a hotel, I stayed with some friends from university. I went sightseeing in the afternoons and I took a lot of photos. My favourite place was the Blue Mosque – it's very beautiful. I was only in Turkey for a week, so I didn't visit any other places. Next time, maybe!

Jeff

Last year I travelled around Colombia, in South America. My favourite place was Cartagena, a beautiful old city by the sea. I stayed in a nice hotel and went to the beach every afternoon. I also visited Providencia Island – the beaches there are fantastic. But I didn't go swimming because I can't swim!

Bob and Liz

We didn't go on holiday last year, but two years ago we went to China. Our favourite place was Guilin – the scenery is amazing. We stayed in a small hotel and went for a walk every morning. We also rented a car and visited some beautiful places. We only stayed in Guilin for four days, but we took 300 photos!

Help with Grammar Past Simple: negative

 a) Look at these sentences. Notice the word order.

I	didn't	stay	in a hotel.
She	didn't	visit	any other places.

(didn't = did not)

b) Write these sentences in the table.

1 He **didn't go** swimming.
2 We **didn't go** on holiday last year.

G9.2 p117

Guilin

Cartagena

Istanbul

7 Cover the texts. Then answer these questions.

1 Where did Nancy go on holiday?
2 Who did she stay with?
3 When did Jeff go to the beach?
4 Did he go swimming?
5 Did Bob and Liz visit China last year?
6 How many photos did they take?

Help with Grammar
Past Simple: questions and short answers

8 *WH-* QUESTIONS (?)

a) Look at these questions. Notice the word order.

Where	did	Nancy	go	on holiday?
Who	did	she	stay	with?

b) Write these questions in the table.

1 When **did** he **go** to the beach?
2 How many photos **did** they **take**?

c) Fill in the gaps with *did* or *didn't*.

YES / NO QUESTIONS (?)	SHORT ANSWERS
Did he go swimming?	Yes, he did. No, he ....
.... they visit China last year?	Yes, they .... No, they didn't.

G9.3 p117

9 [R9.9] [P] Listen and practise the questions and short answers in **8**.

10 Work in pairs. Student A → p91. Student B → p97.

Get ready ... Get it right!

11 a) Make Past Simple questions with *you*.

● When ... last go on holiday?
  When did you last go on holiday?
● Where ... go?
● What ... do there?
● Who ... go with?
● Where ... stay?
● How ... travel around?
● ... have a good time?

b) Answer the questions for you.

12 a) Work in pairs. Ask your partner the questions.

b) Tell the class about your partner's holiday.

5 [R9.8] [P] Listen and practise the sentences in **4**.

6 a) Make these sentences negative. Write the correct sentences.

1 a) Nancy went to Paris.
   Nancy didn't go to Paris. She went to Istanbul.
   b) She went sightseeing in the mornings.
2 a) Jeff travelled around Colombia two years ago.
   b) He stayed with friends.
3 a) Bob and Liz stayed in a big hotel.
   b) They rented bikes.

b) Work in pairs. Compare sentences.

73

Vocabulary at the station
Real World buying train tickets
Help with Listening sentence stress (3)
Review holiday activities; Past Simple

QUICK REVIEW ● ● ●
Write four things people do on holiday (*stay in a hotel, rent a car*, etc.).
Work in pairs. Compare lists. Then talk about your favourite holiday:
A *Two years ago I went to Japan.* **B** *Where did you stay?*

Two days in Liverpool

1 **a)** Write four sentences about things you did last weekend.

b) Work in pairs. Tell your partner about your weekend. Ask questions.

> I went out with friends on Saturday.

> Where did you go?

> We went to the cinema.

> What did you see?

c) Tell the class two things your partner did last weekend.

2 **a)** Look at photos A and B. What do you know about Liverpool?

b) **R9.10** It's Monday morning. Look at photo C. Listen to Caroline and James. When did Caroline go to Liverpool? Did she have a good time?

c) Listen again. Choose the correct words.

1 James *went out* / ~~didn't go out~~ last weekend.
2 Caroline took a lot of photos on *Saturday* / *Sunday*.
3 Caroline and Paul went to a *Japanese* / *Chinese* restaurant.
4 They stayed with Paul's *sister* / *brother*.
5 They went to the Cavern Club on Sunday *morning* / *afternoon*.
6 They travelled to Liverpool by *plane* / *train*.

d) Work in pairs. Compare answers.

Liverpool

The CAVERN CLUB

James   Caroline

Help with Listening Sentence stress (3)

3 **a)** **R9.10** Read and listen to the beginning of the conversation. Notice the sentence stress. We stress the important words.

CAROLINE Héllo, Jámes. Did you háve a goód weekénd?

JAMES Hi, Cároline. Yés, I díd, thánks. I dídn't gó óut, I stáyed at hóme áll weekénd and wátched TV. Whát about yoú? Whát did yoú dó?

CAROLINE Paúl and I wént to Líverpool.

b) Look at R9.10, p125. Listen again and notice the sentence stress.

At the station

4 **a)** Look at the photos. Match these words to 1–6.

> a customer *1*   a single   a return   a ticket office
> a ticket machine   a platform

b) [R9.11] [P] Listen and practise.

Real World   Buying train tickets

5 **a)** [R9.12] It's Saturday morning. James is at the station. Listen and fill in the gaps in this conversation.

CUSTOMER	TICKET SELLER
Two returns to a) *Liverpool* , please.	
	When do you want to come back?
Tomorrow evening.	
	OK. That's b)£_____ , please. Here are your tickets.
Thanks. What time's the next train?	
	There's one at c)_____ .
Which platform?	
	Platform d)_____ .
What time does it arrive in Liverpool?	
	At e)_____ .
Thanks a lot. Bye.	

b) Work in pairs. Compare answers.

[RW9.1] p117

6 [R9.13] [P] Listen and practise the sentences in 5a).

Two returns to Liverpool, please.

7 **a)** Work in pairs. Practise the conversation in 5a). Take turns to be the customer.

b) Close your books. Practise the conversation again.

8 **a)** Read this conversation. Choose the correct words.

CUSTOMER   A single ¹(*to*) / *from* Oxford, please.
TICKET SELLER   OK. ²*That* / *That's* £18.60, please. Here's ³*you* / *your* ticket.
C   Thanks. What time's the ⁴*next* / *near* train?
TS   There's one ⁵*at* / *on* 11.52.
C   ⁶*Which* / *Where* platform?
TS   Platform 1.
C   What time ⁷*do* / *does* it arrive in Oxford?
TS   ⁸*In* / *At* 12.47.
C   Thanks ⁹*much* / *a lot*. Bye.

b) [R9.14] Listen and check.

c) Work in pairs. Practise the conversation. Take turns to be the customer.

9 Work in new pairs. Student A → p91. Student B → p97.

9D # Who, what, when?

Vocabulary question words
Review questions in the present
and the past; big numbers

QUICK REVIEW ●●●
Work in pairs. Ask questions about last weekend. Find five things that you both did:
A *Did you eat out last weekend?*
B *Yes, I did.* A *Me too.*

1 a) Check these words with your teacher.

> the moon   sink   an explorer
> climb   a cab

b) Work in pairs. Do the quiz.

c) Check your answers on p126. How many are correct?

Help with Vocabulary
Question words

2 Look again at the words in **bold** in the quiz. Match the question words to the things they ask about.

Who — a thing
What — a person
When   a reason (*because*)
Where   a number
Why   a place
How old   a time
How many   age
How much   an amount of money (£50, etc.)

V9.4 p116

3 Work in pairs. Student A → p86. Student B → p92.

4 a) Write four questions. Use the question words in 2.

b) Work in new pairs. Take turns to ask your questions. Ask more questions if possible.

c) Tell the class two things about your partner.

The Travel Quiz

1 Who was the first man to walk on the moon?
a) Buzz Aldrin
b) Louis Armstrong
c) Neil Armstrong

2 What is the name of the train from Moscow to Beijing?
a) The Trans-Asian Express
b) The Trans-Siberian Express
c) The Orient Express

3 When did the Titanic sink?
a) In 1912.
b) In 1922.
c) In 1932.

4 Where was the famous explorer Christopher Columbus born?
a) In Italy.
b) In Portugal.
c) In Spain.

5 Why can't you rent a car on the island of Sark?
a) Because there aren't any people.
b) Because there aren't any roads.
c) Because there aren't any cars.

6 How old was Sir Edmund Hillary when he climbed Everest in 1953?
a) 33
b) 43
c) 53

7 How many yellow cabs are there in New York City?
a) About 7,000.
b) About 13,000.
c) About 20,000.

8 How much was a Rolls-Royce Silver Ghost in 1907?
a) About £500.
b) About £1,000.
c) About £1,500.

Help with Sounds /l/ and /r/

1 a) **R9.15** Look at the pictures. Listen to the sounds and words.

/l/

leave

/r/

arrive

b) **P** Listen again and practise.

2 a) **R9.16** Listen to these words. Notice how we say the pink and blue consonants.

| /l/ | leave plane flying like
England place dollars holiday
wallet travelling classroom |

| /r/ | arrive train read write price
Russia around very married
travelling classroom |

b) **P** Listen again and practise.

3 a) Sometimes we don't say the letter r in British English. Look at these words. Which rs do we say? Which don't we say?

friend ✓ first ✗ doctor green

morning radio sport park

right theatre fruit start

tomorrow great terrible

b) **R9.17** **P** Listen and check. Listen again and practise.

9 Review   Language Summary 9, p116

1 a) Find eight words for transport. **V9.1**

b) Work in pairs. Say when you use the transport in **1a**).

2 a) Write the Past Simple of these verbs. Which three verbs are regular? **G9.1**

~~get up~~ leave watch have
start buy play go

get up → got up

b) Fill in the gaps with the Past Simple of the verbs in **2a**).

Yesterday …
1 I *got up* at 7 a.m.
2 I .... home at 8 a.m.
3 I .... work at 9 a.m.
4 I .... pasta for lunch.
5 I .... some new clothes.
6 I .... to the cinema.
7 I .... TV after dinner.
8 I .... computer games.

c) Tick (✓) the sentences in **2b**) that are true for you. Then compare sentences in pairs.

3 a) Match the verb in A to a word or phrase in B. **V9.2**

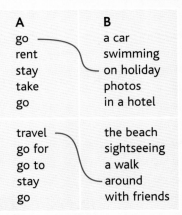

A	B
go	a car
rent	swimming
stay	on holiday
take	photos
go	in a hotel

travel	the beach
go for	sightseeing
go to	a walk
stay	around
go	with friends

b) Work in pairs. Say what you did and didn't do on your last holiday. **G9.2**

I went on holiday to Italy.
I didn't rent a car.

4 a) Make questions with these words. **G9.3**

1 early / you / get up / today / Did ?
2 last Sunday / do / What / you / did ?
3 last weekend / you / shopping / Did / go ?
4 for breakfast / have / you / today / did / What ?

b) Work in pairs. Ask and answer the questions in **4a**).

5 a) Write the words. **RW9.1**

C   Two ¹*singles* to Bath, please.
TS OK. That's £34.20, please. Here are your ²t.......... .
C   Thanks. What time's the ³n.......... train?
TS ⁴T.......... one at 3.15.
C   Which ⁵p.......... ?
TS ⁶P.......... 2.
C   What time does it ⁷a.......... in Bath?
TS At 4.50.
C   Thanks a lot. Bye.

b) Work in pairs. Practise the conversation.

Progress Portfolio

a) Tick (✓) the things you can do in English.

☐ I can talk about transport.
☐ I can talk about the past.
☐ I can understand a simple article.
☐ I can talk about things I do on holiday.
☐ I can ask and answer questions about the past.
☐ I can buy train tickets.
☐ I can use question words.

b) What do you need to study again? **⦿ 9A–D**

10 My future

10A Life changes

Vocabulary future plans; future time phrases
Grammar *be going to*: positive and negative
Review question words

QUICK REVIEW ●●●
Write four questions with question words (*What, How many*, etc.). Work in pairs. Ask your questions. Ask more questions if possible: **A** *What did you do last night?* **B** *I went out with friends.* **A** *Where did you go?*

Future plans

 1 a) Work in pairs. Fill in the gaps with these verbs. Then check in **V10.1** p118.

~~start~~ look for get do leave move

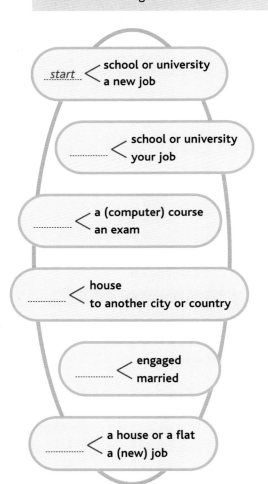

start < school or university / a new job

.... < school or university / your job

.... < a (computer) course / an exam

.... < house / to another city or country

.... < engaged / married

.... < a house or a flat / a (new) job

b) **R10.1** **P** Listen and practise.

c) Work in pairs. Test your partner.

(a course) (do a course)

A world language

 2 a) **R10.2** Look at the photos. Read and listen to Sabrina, Carmen, Luca and Wing Yu. Where does each person study English?

b) Read the texts again. Fill in the gaps with *Sabrina, Carmen, Luca* and *Wing Yu*.

1 *Luca* 's going to get married.
2 ....'s going to do a computer course.
3 ....'s going to travel around the UK.
4 ....'s going to move to Miami.
5 ....'s going to look for a job.
6 ....'s going to start a new job.
7 ....'s going to move to Rome.

c) Work in pairs. Compare answers.

Sabrina from Germany

I do English at school – it's my favourite subject. I'm going to leave school in June, but I'm not going to start university this year. First I'm going to do a computer course, then I'm going to look for a job in the UK.

Carmen from Mexico

My husband, Ed, is American, so we sometimes speak English at home. I also study English online. Our two sons are going to move to Mexico City in September. And next year Ed's going to leave his job and we're going to move to Miami!

Help with Grammar *be going to*: positive and negative

- We use *be going to* + verb to talk about future plans.

3 **a)** Look at these sentences. Notice the word order. Which sentence is negative?

I	'm	going to	do	a computer course.
Ed	's	going to	leave	his job.
We	aren't	going to	stay	here.

b) Write these sentences in the table. Which sentence is negative?

1 We're going to **travel** around the UK.
2 I'm **not** going to **start** university this year.

G10.1 p119

4 **R10.3** **P** Listen and practise the sentences in **3**.

I'm gŏing to /tə/ dŏ a compŭter cŏurse.

Luca from Italy

I study English at the University of Bologna. My girlfriend, Silvia, is also a student there. We're going to get married next year. But we aren't going to stay here, we're going to move to Rome.

5 **a)** Fill in the gaps with the correct form of *be going to* and the verbs in brackets.

1 a) We *'re going to buy* a house near the beach. (buy)
  b) Our sons _____ a flat together. (look for)
2 a) We _____ a big wedding. (not have)
  b) She _____ university next year. (leave)
3 a) He _____ in the UK for two weeks. (stay)
  b) We _____ Bath and Cambridge. (visit)
4 a) I _____ my exams in June. (do)
  b) I _____ a job in London. (not look for)

b) Work in pairs. Compare answers. Then match the sentences to the people in the photos.

Future time phrases

6 **a)** Put these future time phrases in order.

a) in 2025   d) next month
b) tonight *1*   e) tomorrow morning
c) in December   f) next week

b) Write three sentences about things that your family and friends are going to do in the future. Use phrases from **6a)** and your own ideas.

My sister Helena is going to move house in March.

c) Work in pairs. Tell your partner your sentences.

Get ready ... Get it right!

7 Write one thing you're going to do: after class, tomorrow evening, next Sunday, next week, next month, next year.

meet some friends after class

8 **a)** Work in groups. Talk about your plans. Are any the same?

I'm going to meet some friends after class.   Me too.

b) Tell the class about your group's plans.

Lin and I are going to meet some friends after class.

Wing Yu from China

I'm at an English language school in London. We have classes for five hours every day! Next month my brother is going to visit me and we're going to travel around the UK. Then I'm going to start a new job in Shanghai.

What are you going to do?

QUICK REVIEW ● ● ●
Write one phrase for these verbs: *start, leave, do, move, get, look for* (*start a new job*, etc.). Work in pairs. Compare phrases. Then say when you are going to do some of the things on your lists: *I'm going to start a new job next month.*

> **Vocabulary** phrases with *have, watch, go, go to*
> **Grammar** *be going to*: questions and short answers
> **Review** future plans; *be going to*: positive and negative

Phrases with *have, watch, go, go to*

 1 a) Match these words or phrases to the correct verbs. Then check in V10.3 p118.

> dinner with friends   the cinema
> shopping   TV   swimming   the news
> coffee with friends   sport on TV
> the gym   running   a party (x 2)

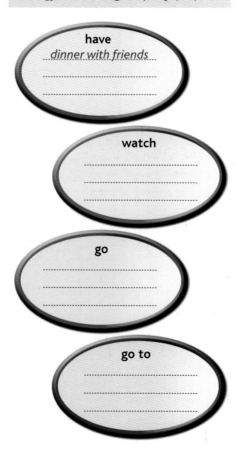

have
dinner with friends
_____
_____
_____

watch
_____
_____
_____

go
_____
_____
_____

go to
_____
_____
_____

b) R10.4 P Listen and practise.

c) Work in pairs. Write one more word or phrase for the verbs in **1a)**.

have breakfast   go to a concert

2 a) Write two true sentences and two false sentences about your future plans. Use *be going to* and phrases from **1**.

I'm going to have a party on Saturday.

b) Work in pairs. Say your sentences. Guess if your partner's sentences are true or false.

A new start

 3 a) R10.5 Look at the photo and listen to the conversation. What are Darla, Liam and Wesley going to do on Saturday?

b) Listen again. Answer these questions.

1 When's Darla going to move to Australia?
2 What's her husband going to do there?
3 Is Darla going to look for a job?
4 Where are Darla's sisters going to live?
5 Are Darla and Justin going to have a party?
6 What's Liam going to do this evening?

> **Help with Grammar** *be going to*: questions and short answers

 4 *WH-* QUESTIONS (?)

a) Look at these questions. Notice the word order.

When	's	Darla	going to	move	to Australia?
What	's	her husband	going to	do	there?

b) Write these questions in the table.

1 Where **are** Darla's sisters going to **live**?
2 What's Liam going to **do** this evening?

c) Fill in the gaps with *am, is, are, isn't* and *aren't*.

YES / NO QUESTIONS (?)	SHORT ANSWERS
Are you going to watch a film?	Yes, I _____ . / No, I'm not.
_____ she going to look for a job?	Yes, she is. / No, she _____ .
_____ you going to sell your flat?	Yes, we _____ . / No, we aren't.
_____ they going to have a party?	Yes, they are. / No, they _____ .

G10.2 p119

Liam

Darla

Wesley

5 **a)** Make questions with these words.

1 are / What / next weekend / going to / you / do ?
What are you going to do next weekend?
2 after class / are / going to / you / What / do ?
3 going to / you / When / your homework / do / are ?
4 get up / are / going to / you / tomorrow / What time ?
5 you / tomorrow evening / are / Where / dinner / have / going to ?
6 going to / you / next year / go / are / on holiday / Where ?

b) R10.6 P Listen and check. Listen again and practise.

Whát are you góing to /tə/ dó néxt weekénd?

c) Work in pairs. Ask and answer the questions in 5a).
Make notes on your partner's answers.

d) Work in new pairs. Talk about your partner in 5c).

Get ready ...
Get it right!

6 Write *yes / no* questions with *you* for these plans. Use *be going to* and verbs from **1a)**.

- shopping on Saturday?
  Are you going to go shopping on Saturday?
- TV tonight?
- the cinema this week?
- coffee with friends after class?
- swimming or running next weekend?
- the gym next week?
- a party next weekend?
- dinner with friends on Saturday evening?

7 **a)** Ask other students your questions. Find one person who is going to do each thing. Then ask one more question.

> Are you going to go shopping on Saturday?
> Yes, I am.

> What are you going to buy?
> A new suit.

b) Tell the class about one student's plans.

> Yusuf's going to buy a new suit on Saturday.

Good luck!

Vocabulary adjectives (3): feelings
Real World saying goodbye and good luck
Review *be going to*; frequency adverbs

QUICK REVIEW ● ● ●
Think of two things you're going to do after this course. Work in groups. Tell each other your plans. Ask questions if possible: **A** *After this course I'm going to go on holiday.* **B** *Where are you going to go?*

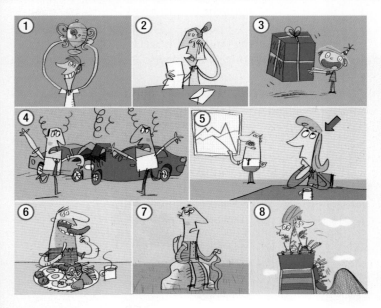

How do you feel?

1 **a)** Match these adjectives to pictures 1–8. Then check in V10.4 p118.

> excited *3*   tired   happy   sad
> bored   scared   hungry   angry

TIP! • We can say *I'm* excited, etc. or *I feel* excited, etc.

b) R10.7 P Listen and practise.

c) Work in pairs. Test your partner.

> Who's bored?   The woman in picture 5.

2 **a)** Complete these sentences with *always, usually, sometimes* or *never* to make them true for you.

1 I'm .... happy on my birthday.
2 I'm .... bored at the weekend.
3 I'm .... angry with my friends.
4 I'm .... tired on Friday evenings.
5 I'm .... hungry at 4 a.m.
6 I'm .... excited before I go on holiday.
7 I'm .... scared when I fly.
8 I'm .... sad when I say goodbye to people.

b) Work in pairs. Compare sentences.

See you soon!

3 **a)** Read conversations 1–3. Match them to photos A–C.

1

WILL   Right, it's time to go. That's my ¹train / flight.
DAD   OK, Will. Have a good ²journey / holiday!
WILL   Thanks a lot. See you in ³two / three weeks.
MUM   Yes, see you. Bye!

2

MAGDA Are you going to study here next ⁴year / course?
HASAN Yes, I am.
MAGDA Me too. See you in ⁵September / December.
HASAN Yes, see you.
MAGDA And good luck with your new ⁶school / job.
HASAN Thanks a lot.

3

MUM   Come on, Julie. You're going to be late.
JULIE   OK, Mum. I'm ready now. Bye, Dad.
DAD   Bye, Julie. Good luck with your ⁷test / exam.
JULIE   Thanks very much. Have a good ⁸time / day!
DAD   Thanks. See you later.

b) R10.8 Listen and choose the correct words.

c) Work in pairs. Compare answers.

Real World Saying goodbye and good luck

4 **a)** Fill in the gaps with these words.

~~holiday~~   much   lot   exam   see   September

Have a good (_holiday_)!

See you (in _____).

Good luck with your (_____).

Thanks a _____ .

Yes, _____ you.

Thanks very _____ .

b) Which phrase in **bold** in 4a) can you use with these words or phrases?

journey   in two weeks   new job   day   next month
weekend   English test   birthday   on Monday
new school   time

Have a good journey.

RW10.1 p119

5 R10.9 P Listen and practise the sentences in 4.
Hǎve a gǒod hǒliday!

6 **a)** Put conversations A and B in order.

A

ALAN   Have a good time!
ALAN   What are you going to do after work? *1*
ALAN   See you tomorrow.

KERRY Yes, see you. Bye!
KERRY Thanks a lot.
KERRY I'm going to have dinner with friends. *2*

B

SID   Thanks. Oh, and good luck with your new job.
SID   To Bodrum, in Turkey.
SID   I'm going to go on holiday next week.

JAN   Really? Where are you going?
JAN   Thanks a lot.
JAN   Have a good holiday!

b) R10.10 Listen and check.

c) Work in pairs. Practise the conversations in 6a).

7 **a)** Think of two things you're going to do in the future.

b) Work in groups or with the whole class. Talk about your plans. Use sentences from 4.

I'm going to meet some friends after class.

Have a good time!

1 Cross out the wrong word or phrase. **V10.1**

1 **start** *a new job* / *a city* / *school*
2 **leave** *married* / *university* / *your job*
3 **do** *a course* / *a flat* / *an exam*
4 **move** *house* / *to Bath* / *a job*
5 **get** *school* / *engaged* / *married*
6 **look for** *a flat* / *engaged* / *a new job*

2 Fill in the gaps with the positive (+) or negative (–) form of *be going to* and these verbs. **G10.1**

~~watch~~   study   get up
play   stay   eat

1 (+) I *'m going to watch* a DVD when I get home.
2 (+) Megan .... tennis next Saturday.
3 (+) I .... in a hotel next weekend.
4 (–) They .... out tonight.
5 (+) We .... English next year.
6 (–) Brian .... early tomorrow.

3 Match a verb in A to a word or phrase in B. **V10.3**

A	B
have	swimming
go to	a party
watch	sport on TV
go	a party
have	running
watch	the gym
go	the news
go to	dinner with friends
watch	shopping
have	TV
go	the cinema
go to	coffee with friends

4 a) Write the missing word in these questions. **G10.2**

going
1 What are you to do tomorrow?
2 Where you going to be next Sunday?
3 Are you going to coffee with friends next weekend?
4 Are you going to study English month?
5 What are you going do after this class?
6 Are going to have a party on your next birthday?

b) Work in pairs. Ask and answer the questions. Ask more questions if possible.

5 a) Find eight adjectives for feelings. (→↓). **V10.4**

H	A	P	P	Y	J	O	S
B	Q	A	N	G	R	Y	A
O	E	X	C	I	T	E	D
R	I	K	G	V	I	S	F
E	H	U	N	G	R	Y	M
D	E	A	J	L	E	N	B
S	C	A	R	E	D	U	C

b) Work in pairs. Mime the adjectives in **5a)**. Guess your partner's adjectives.

Progress Portfolio

a) Tick (✓) the things you can do in English.

☐ I can talk about my future plans.
☐ I can use future time phrases.
☐ I can understand a simple conversation about the future.
☐ I can ask other people about their future plans.
☐ I can say how I feel.
☐ I can say goodbye and good luck.

b) What do you need to study again? **⊙ 10A–C**

Work in groups of four. Read the rules. Then play the game!

Rules

You need: One counter for each student; one dice for each group.

How to play: Put your counters on **START HERE**. Take turns to throw the dice, move your counter and read the instructions on the square. The first student to get to **FINISH** is the winner.

Grammar and **Vocabulary** squares: The first student to land on a Grammar or Vocabulary square answers question 1. The second student to land on the same square answers question 2. If the other students think your answer is correct, you can stay on the square. If the answer is wrong, move back to the last square you were on. If a third or fourth student lands on the same square, he / she can stay on the square without answering a question.

Talk about squares: If you land on a Talk about square, talk about the topic for 15 seconds. If you can't talk for 15 seconds, move back to the last square you were on. If a second or third student lands on the same square, he / she also talks about the same topic for 15 seconds.

Have a rest squares: If you land on a Have a rest square, you stay on the square without answering a question.

End of Course Review

START HERE

1 Fill in the gaps with *'m, 's* or *'re*.
1 I _____ a doctor and she _____ a teacher.
2 He _____ French and they _____ Italian.

2 MOVE FORWARD TWO SQUARES

3 Say the plurals.
1 man, chair, sandwich, person
2 woman, watch, parent, child

4 Talk about your family.

5 Say eight:
1 countries
2 nationalities

6 Make a question.
1 evenings / the / does / What / do / in / he ?
2 you / Sunday / What / did / on / do ?

7 Talk about things you do in your free time.

8 Make a question.
1 there / flat / shops / your / any / near / Are ?
2 are / tomorrow / do / going to / What / you ?

9 MOVE BACK TWO SQUARES

10 Choose the correct words.
1 I *was / were* tired, but she *wasn't / weren't*.
2 Where *did / were* you live when you *did / were* a child?

11 Talk about your daily routine.

12 Make this sentence negative.
1 She likes watching TV.
2 We went out last night.

13 Say eight:
1 jobs
2 places in a town or city

14 HAVE A REST!

15 Choose the correct word.
1 There are *some / any* nice cafés.
2 I love *shop / shopping* for clothes.

16 Talk about things you like and don't like.

17 Say the opposites.
1 hot, cheap, ugly, friendly
2 long, boring, full, easy

18 Say the (+) and (–) short answers.
1 Are they from the UK?
2 Does she work at home?

19 MOVE FORWARD THREE SQUARES

20 Correct this sentence.
1 I didn't went out, I stayed at home.
2 Karen always get up early.

21 HAVE A REST!

22 Talk about places near your home.

23 Which preposition: *in, on* or *at*?
1 the weekend, night, the evening
2 Friday, midday, the morning

24 HAVE A REST!

25 Say these times.
1 7.30, 3.55, 8.00, 2.15
2 6.45, 11.20, 4.35, 12.30

26 Talk about your last holiday.

27 Say six:
1 things people can do online
2 things people do in their free time

28 Talk about what you did last week.

29 Which verb: *do, get* or *have*?
1 a party, a course, married
2 engaged, an exam, coffee with friends

30 Say the Past Simple.
1 buy, travel, get, meet
2 tell, come, visit, leave

31 MOVE BACK THREE SQUARES

32 Say eight:
1 words for food and drink
2 things people do on holiday

33 Talk about things you can and can't do.

34 Correct this question.
1 Where you did go last Saturday?
2 What food do your sister like?

35 Which verb: *go, go to* or *play*?
1 the cinema, shopping, football
2 tennis, concerts, on holiday

36 Choose the correct words.
1 That's *me / my* mum. *She / Her* has two cats.
2 *He / Him* loves soap operas, but I hate *they / them*.

37 MOVE BACK FOUR SQUARES

38 Say the (+) and (–) short answers.
1 Is there a class tomorrow?
2 Did you get up early?

FINISH

Pair and Group Work: Student/Group A

1A ⑩ p7

a) Look at the table. Practise the mobile number and the home number.

	you	your partner
📱	07395 623108	
☎	0161 288 9104	

b) Work with your partner. Ask questions with *What's your … ?*. Write your partner's phone numbers in the table.

c) Check your partner's table. Are the phone numbers correct?

6B ⑦ p49

a) Look at these questions about places near Susan's flat. Fill in the gaps with *Is, Are, a* or *any*. The answers are in brackets ( ).

1   *Is* there *a* post office near Susan's flat? (✓)
2   _____ there _____ good restaurants? (✗)
3   _____ there _____ bus stop? (✓)
4   _____ there _____ museums? (✗)
5   _____ there _____ cashpoint? (✓)

b) Work with your partner. Ask your questions from **a)**. Are your partner's answers correct?

c) Answer your partner's questions. Are your answers correct?

9D ③ p76

a) Work on your own. Choose the correct words.

1   *What* / *Where* did you do yesterday afternoon?
2   *When* / *Who* was your first English teacher?
3   *How old* / *How many* is your best friend?
4   *Why* / *What* do you want to learn English?
5   *Who* / *Where* was your mother born?
6   *When* / *Who* did you last go to the cinema?
7   *How many* / *How much* people live in your house or flat?
8   *How many* / *How much* do you spend on phone calls every month?

b) Work with your partner. Take turns to ask the questions in **a)**. Ask more questions if possible.

> What did you do yesterday afternoon?

> I went shopping.

> What did you buy?

4B ⑧ p33

a) Work on your own. Make questions with the words in column A of the table.

A	B your guess (✓ or ✗)	C your partner's answer (✓ or ✗)
1 a lot / you / Do / eat out ? *Do you eat out a lot?*		
2 DVDs / Do / watch / you ? -------------------------		
3 live / in a house or a flat / you / Do ? -------------------------		
4 Italian food / you / like / Do ? -------------------------		
5 you / Do / a computer / have ? -------------------------		

b) Guess your partner's answers to questions 1–5. Put a tick (✓) or a cross (✗) in column B of the table.

c) Work with your partner. Ask questions 1–5. Put a tick (✓) or a cross (✗) in column C of the table. Are your guesses correct?

> Do you eat out a lot?

> Yes, I do. / No, I don't.

d) Answer your partner's questions.

1B 🔟 p9

a) Look at the photo. Ask about people 1, 3 and 5. Write the names and countries.

> Number 1. What's his name?

> Where's he from?

b) Answer your partner's questions about people 2, 4 and 6.

c) Look at the photo for one minute. Remember the people's names and countries.

d) Close your books. Ask and answer questions about the people.

> Where's David from?

> He's from the UK.

1 **Name** _____
  Country _____

2 **Name** ___David___
  Country ___the UK___

3 **Name** _____
  Country _____

4 **Name** ___Nina___
  Country ___Italy___

5 **Name** _____
  Country _____

6 **Name** ___Polly___
  Country ___The USA___

2B 9️⃣ p17

a) Look at these photos of Ben's friends. Write *yes / no* questions to check the information in **blue** about Roberto, Wendy and Alex.

Is Roberto Spanish?

b) Work with your partner. Ask your questions from **a)**. Tick (✓) the correct information. Change the wrong information.

c) Answer your partner's questions about Silvio, Yi Chen and Omar.

> Is Silvio Italian?

> No, he isn't. He's Brazilian.

d) Compare answers with another student A.

> Roberto isn't Spanish. He's Mexican.

name	Roberto	Wendy	Alex
nationality	Spanish?	American?	Russian?
	....	....	....
job	a police officer?	a waitress?	a teacher?
	....	....	....
married or single	married?	married?	married?
	....	....	....

name	Silvio	Yi Chen	Omar
nationality	Brazilian	Chinese	Egyptian
job	a taxi driver	a shop assistant	an actor
married or single	married	married	single

3A 13 p23

Sally and Dan

a) Work on your own. Choose the correct words.

1 Where *is* / *(are)* Sally and Dan?
2 *Is* / *Are* the people very friendly?
3 *Is* / *Are* Sally and Dan in an old hotel?
4 Where *'s* / *are* the hotel?
5 *Is* / *Are* the rooms very big?
6 *Is* / *Are* it very cold?

b) Check the answers in email A on p22.

c) Work with your partner. Ask your questions about Sally and Dan in **a)**. Are his / her answers correct?

d) Answer your partner's questions about Fiona and Nick. Don't look at p23!

8B 10 p65

a) Work on your own. Fill in the gaps with *was* or *were*.

1 Where __was__ the last wedding you went* to?
2 When _____ it?
3 Who _____ the bride and groom?
4 How many people _____ at the wedding?
5 _____ the food good?
6 _____ any of your friends there?
7 _____ there a party after the wedding?
8 _____ there any music?

went = Past Simple of go

b) Work with your partner. Ask your questions from **a)**. Make notes on his / her answers.

c) Answer your partner's questions about the last party you went to.

d) Work with another student A. Tell him / her about the wedding your partner went to.

4C 10 p35

a) You are a customer. Your partner is a shop assistant. Buy things a)–d) from your partner's shop. You start. How much do you spend?

> Excuse me. Do you have any ... ?
> How much is this ... , please?
> How much are these ... , please?
> Can I have ... , please?
> No, that's all, thanks.
> Here you are.

b) You are a shop assistant. Your partner is a customer. He / She wants to buy things 1–4. Have a conversation with your partner. Your partner starts.

> Yes, they're over there.
> It's £... .
> They're ...p each.
> Sure. Anything else?
> OK, that's £... .

4D 8 p36

a) Look at these film times. Work with your partner. Take turns to ask the times of the films. Write the times.

> What time is 'The Italian Teacher' on?

> It's on at quarter past four, ...

Film times

The Italian Teacher	4.15	....	....
Seven Sisters	2.55	5.15	8.50
Married or Single?	....	7.20	....
Beautiful Day	3.30	5.45	9.05
Monday to Friday	3.05	....	....
The Actor's Wife	3.45	6.50	9.15

b) Check the times with your partner. Are they correct?

5A 8 p39

a) Work on your own. Fill in the gaps in the questions in column A of the table. Use *Do* and these verbs.

> ~~get up~~   have   sleep   drink   watch

A	B your partner's answer (✓ or ✗)
1 _Do_ you _get up_ before seven o'clock?	
2 .... you .... TV in the morning?	
3 .... you .... breakfast in a café?	
4 .... you .... a lot of coffee?	
5 .... you .... in the day?	

b) Work with your partner. Ask questions 1–5. Put a tick (✓) or a cross (✗) in column B of the table.

> Do you get up before seven o'clock?

> Yes, I do. / No, I don't. I get up at about eight.

c) Answer your partner's questions. Give more information if possible.

d) Work with another student A. Tell him / her about your partner.

> Uli gets up at about eight.

5B 8 p41

a) Work on your own. Fill in the gaps in these questions about Nadine's routine. Use *does she* and the correct prepositions.

1 What time _does_ _she_ get up _in_ the week?
2 What .... do ...... Wednesday afternoon?
3 .... have classes ...... Friday morning?
4 .... go out with friends ...... the weekend?
5 .... phone her mother ...... Sunday evening?

b) Work with your partner. Ask your partner the questions in **a)**.

c) Look at pictures a)–e). Then answer your partner's questions.

the week

Wednesday evening

the weekend

Sunday evening

6C 7 p51

a) Look at the questions about Bath in column A of the table. Fill in the gaps with these words.

~~have~~   Where's   on   show   much   open

A	B
1 a) Do you _have_ a map of England?	a) yes / no
b) How _____ is it?	b) £_____
2 a) When is the American Museum _____ ?	a) from _____ to _____
b) Is it closed _____ Mondays?	b) yes / no
3 a) _____ the Odeon cinema?	
b) Can you _____ me on this map?	

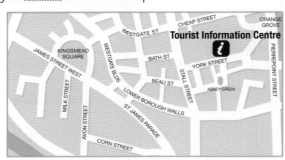

b) You are a tourist in Bath. Your partner works at the tourist information centre. Ask the questions in column A of the table. Write the answers in column B and on the map.

Good morning.   Hello, can I help you?

Yes, please. Do you have ... ?

c) You work at the tourist information centre in Bath. Your partner is a tourist. Answer his / her questions. Use this information.

d) Check your partner's answers. Are they correct?

7A 10 p55

a) Work on your own. Write questions with *Do you like* … ? for the things in column A of the table.

1 Do you like playing computer games?

A	B (✓ X)	C (✓ X)
1		
2		
3		
4		
5		
6		

b) Work on your own. Guess if your partner likes the things in the table. Put a tick (✓) or a cross (✗) in column B of the table.

c) Work with your partner. Ask your questions from **a)**. Put a tick (✓) or a cross (✗) in column C of the table. Are your guesses correct?

d) Answer your partner's questions.

e) Tell the class two things about your partner.

Marcelo loves playing computer games. He doesn't like horror films.

7B ⑩ p57

a) Work on your own. Look at the things Ella and Daniel can and can't do. Write questions with *Can* for the **pink** gaps in the table.

1 Can Ella speak German?

		Ella	Daniel
1	Guten Tag!		✗
2	🎹	✓	
3	🎸		✓
4	🚲	✓	
5	🎿		✗
6	🏊	✓	
7	🎾		✗
8	🏀		✗

b) Work with your partner. Take turns to ask your questions from **a)**. Fill in the gaps in the table with a tick (✓) or a cross (✗). You start.

c) Compare tables with your partner. What can both children do?

9B ⑩ p73

a) Work on your own. Make questions about Nancy with the words in column A of the table.

A	B Nancy	C Jeff
1 she / What / every morning / do / did ? *What did she do every morning?*		(go) sightseeing
2 any museums / visit / she / Did ? ------		✗
3 in the evenings / she / do / did / What ? ------		(have) dinner in his hotel
4 she / did / travel around / How ? ------		(rent) a car
5 buy / Did / presents for her family / she ? ------		✓

b) Work with your partner. Ask your questions from **a)** about Nancy. Write the answers in column B of the table.

c) Look at column C. Answer your partner's questions about Jeff. Use the Past Simple form of the verbs in brackets.

9C ⑨ p75

a) You are at a station. You want to buy these tickets. Your partner is a ticket seller. Ask your partner questions and complete the table. The time now is 9 a.m.

ticket	price	time of next train	platform	time train arrives
two returns to Bath (you want to come back tomorrow)				
two singles to Bristol				

b) You are a ticket seller. Your partner wants to buy some tickets. Look at this information. Answer your partner's questions.

place	price	time of next train	platform	time train arrives
Birmingham	single: £28.20 return: £42.50	10.10	2	11.39
Manchester	single: £43.40 return: £55.80	9.25	5	12.41

Pair and Group Work: Student/Group B

1A 10 p7

a) Look at the table. Practise the mobile number and the home number.

	you	your partner
📱	07902 715843	
☎	020 7911 6047	

b) Work with your partner. Ask questions with *What's your … ?*. Write your partner's phone numbers in the table.

c) Check your partner's table. Are the phone numbers correct?

6B 7 p49

a) Look at these questions about places near Susan's flat. Fill in the gaps with *Is*, *Are*, *a* or *any*. The answers are in brackets ( ).

1 *Is* there *a* station near Susan's flat? (✗)
2 _____ there _____ shops? (✓)
3 _____ there _____ chemist's? (✓)
4 _____ there _____ nice cafés? (✗)
5 _____ there _____ supermarket? (✓)

b) Work with your partner. Answer your partner's questions. Are your answers correct?

c) Ask your questions from **a)**. Are your partner's answers correct?

9D 3 p76

a) Work on your own. Choose the correct words.

1 (What)/ *Where* did you do last night?
2 *When / Who* is your best friend?
3 *How old / How many* is your mobile phone?
4 *Why / What* did you come to this school?
5 *Who / Where* was your father born?
6 *When / Who* did you last go to a concert?
7 *How many / How much* brothers and sisters do you have?
8 *How many / How much* do you spend on travel every month?

b) Work with your partner. Take turns to ask the questions in **a)**. Ask more questions if possible.

> What did you do last night?

> I went out with some friends.

> Where did you go?

4B 8 p33

a) Work on your own. Make questions with the words in column A of the table.

A	B your guess (✓ or ✗)	C your partner's answer (✓ or ✗)
a) watch / you / Do / a lot / TV ? *Do you watch TV a lot?*		
b) tennis or football / Do / play / you ?		
c) you / in an office / work / Do ?		
d) like / Do / Chinese food / you ?		
e) have / a dog or a cat / you / Do ?		

b) Guess your partner's answers to questions a)–e). Put a tick (✓) or a cross (✗) in column B of the table.

c) Work with your partner. Answer his / her questions.

d) Ask questions a)–e). Put a tick (✓) or a cross (✗) in column C of the table. Are your guesses correct?

> Do you watch TV a lot?

> Yes, I do. / No, I don't.

1B ⑩ p9

a) Look at the photo. Answer your partner's questions about people 1, 3 and 5.

b) Ask about people 2, 4 and 6. Write the names and countries.

> Number 2. What's his name?

> Where's he from?

c) Look at the photo for one minute. Remember the people's names and countries.

d) Close your books. Ask and answer questions about the people.

> Where's Sue from?

> She's from Australia.

1 **Name** _Adam_
   Country _Germany_

2 **Name** ....
   Country ....

3 **Name** _Mario_
   Country _Spain_

4 **Name** ....
   Country ....

5 **Name** _Sue_
   Country _Australia_

6 **Name** ....
   Country ....

2B ⑨ p17

a) Look at these photos of Ben's friends. Write *yes / no* questions to check the information in **blue** about Silvio, Yi Chen and Omar.

Is Silvio Italian?

b) Work with your partner. Answer his / her questions about Roberto, Wendy and Alex.

> Is Roberto Spanish?

> No, he isn't. He's Mexican.

c) Ask your partner your questions from **a)**. Tick (✓) the correct information. Change the wrong information.

d) Compare answers with another student B.

> Silvio isn't Italian. He's Brazilian.

name	Silvio	Yi Chen	Omar
nationality	Italian?	Japanese?	Egyptian?
job	a taxi driver?	a musician?	a doctor?
married or single	married?	married?	married?

name	Roberto	Wendy	Alex
nationality	Mexican	British	Russian
job	a police officer	a waitress	a manager
married or single	single	single	married

3A 13 p23

Fiona and Nick

a) Work on your own. Choose the correct words.

1 Where *is* / *are* Fiona and Nick?
2 *Is* / *Are* the people very friendly?
3 *Is* / *Are* Fiona and Nick in a big hotel?
4 Where *'s* / *are* the hotel?
5 *Is* / *Are* the rooms very nice?
6 *Is* / *Are* the hotel cheap?

b) Check the answers in email B on p23.

c) Work with your partner. Answer your partner's questions about Sally and Dan. Don't look at p22!

d) Ask your questions about Fiona and Nick in **a)**. Are your partner's answers correct?

8B 10 p65

a) Work on your own. Fill in the gaps with *was* or *were*.

1 Where ..*was*.. the last party you went* to?
2 .... it a friend's party?
3 How many people .... at the party?
4 .... any of your family there?
5 When .... the party?
6 .... there any interesting people?
7 .... the music good?
8 .... there any food?

*went = Past Simple of *go*

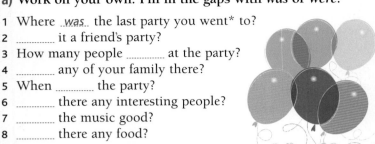

b) Work with your partner. Answer his / her questions about the last wedding you went to.

c) Ask your partner your questions from **a)**. Make notes on his / her answers.

d) Work with another student B. Tell him / her about the party your partner went to.

4C 10 p35

a) You are a shop assistant. Your partner is a customer. He / She wants to buy things a)–d). Have a conversation with your partner. Your partner starts.

> Yes, they're over there.
> It's £... .
> They're £... each.
> Sure. Anything else?
> OK, that's £... .

b) You are a customer. Your partner is a shop assistant. Buy things 1–4 from your partner's shop. You start. How much do you spend?

> Excuse me. Do you have any ... ?
> How much is this ... , please?
> How much are these ... , please?
> Can I have ... , please?
> No, that's all, thanks.
> Here you are.

4D ⑧ p36

a) Look at these film times. Work with your partner. Take turns to ask the times of the films. Write the times.

> What time is 'Seven Sisters' on?

> It's on at five to three, ...

Film times

The Italian Teacher	4.15	7.00	9.25
Seven Sisters	2.55	....	....
Married or Single?	4.25	7.20	9.10
Beautiful Day	....	5.45	....
Monday to Friday	3.05	4.50	6.45
The Actor's Wife	....	....	9.15

b) Check the times with your partner. Are they correct?

5A ⑧ p39

a) Work on your own. Fill in the gaps in the questions in column A of the table. Use *Do* and these verbs.

> ~~get~~   eat   work   go   have

A	B your partner's answer (✓ or ✗)
a) *Do* you *get* home after six o'clock?	
b) .... you .... dinner before nine?	
c) .... you .... to bed after midnight?	
d) .... you .... at the weekend?	
e) .... you .... a lot of fruit?	

b) Work with your partner. Answer his / her questions. Give more information if possible.

c) Ask your partner questions a)–e). Put a tick (✓) or a cross (✗) in column B of the table.

> Do you get home after six o'clock?

> Yes, I do. / No, I don't. I get home at about five.

d) Work with another student B. Tell him / her about your partner.

> Kwan gets home at about five.

5B ⑧ p41

a) Work on your own. Fill in the gaps in these questions about Nadine's routine. Use *does she* and the correct prepositions.

1 What time *does* *she* go to bed *in* the week?
2 .... have classes ...... Tuesday morning?
3 What .... do ...... Wednesday evening?
4 What time .... get up ...... the weekend?
5 .... eat out ...... Sunday evening?

b) Work with your partner. Look at pictures a)–e). Then answer your partner's questions.

c) Ask your partner the questions in a).

the week

Wednesday afternoon

the weekend

Sunday evening

6C ⑦ p51

a) Look at the questions about Bath in column A of the table. Fill in the gaps with these words.

~~have~~ Where's on show much open

A	B
1 a) Do you _have_ a guide book of Bath? b) How _____ is it?	a) yes / no b) £_____
2 a) When is the Building of Bath Museum _____ ? b) Is it closed _____ Mondays?	a) from _____ to _____ b) yes / no
3 a) _____ the SouthGate shopping centre? b) Can you _____ me on this map?	

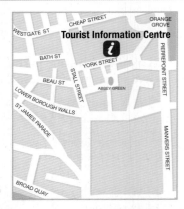

b) You work at the tourist information centre in Bath. Your partner is a tourist. Answer his / her questions. Use this information.

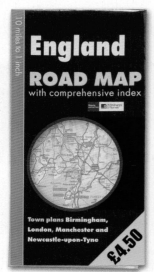

England ROAD MAP with comprehensive index

Town plans Birmingham, London, Manchester and Newcastle-upon-Tyne £4.50

THE AMERICAN MUSEUM
Opening hours
(Tuesday–Sunday)
12.00–5.00 p.m.
Closed on Mondays

c) You are a tourist in Bath. Your partner works at the tourist information centre. Ask the questions in column A of the table. Write the answers in column B and on the map.

(Good morning.) (Hello, can I help you?)

(Yes, please. Do you have ... ?)

d) Check your partner's answers. Are they correct?

7A ⑩ p55

a) Work on your own. Write questions with *Do you like … ?* for the things in column A of the table.

a) Do you like Chinese food?

A	B (✓ ✗)	C (✓ ✗)
a)		
b)		
c)		
d)		
e)		
f)		

b) Work on your own. Guess if your partner likes the things in the table. Put a tick (✓) or a cross (✗) in column B of the table.

c) Work with your partner. Answer his / her questions.

d) Ask your questions from a). Put a tick (✓) or a cross (✗) in column C of the table. Are your guesses correct?

e) Tell the class two things about your partner.

(Laura doesn't like Chinese food. She loves visiting new places.)

7B 🔟 p57

a) Work on your own. Look at the things Ella and Daniel can and can't do. Write questions with *Can* for the **pink** gaps in the table.

1 Can Daniel speak German?

	Ella	Daniel
1 Guten Tag!	✓	
2 (piano)		✗
3 (guitar)	✗	
4 (bicycle)		✓
5 (skis)	✗	
6 (swimming pool)		✓
7 (tennis)	✓	
8 (basketball)		✗

b) Work with your partner. Take turns to ask your questions from a). Fill in the gaps in the table with a tick (✓) or a cross (✗). Your partner starts.

c) Compare tables with your partner. What can both children do?

9B 🔟 p73

a) Work on your own. Make questions about Jeff with the words in column A of the table.

A	B	C
	Jeff	Nancy
1 he / What / every morning / do / did ? *What did he do every morning?*		(go) for a walk
2 any museums / visit / he / Did ?		✓
3 in the evenings / he / do / did / What ?		(have) dinner with her friends
4 he / did / travel around / How ?		(go) by bus and taxi
5 buy / Did / presents for his family / he ?		✗

b) Work with your partner. Look at column C. Answer his / her questions about Nancy. Use the Past Simple form of the verbs in brackets.

c) Ask your partner questions from a) about Jeff. Write the answers in column B of the table.

9C 9️⃣ p75

a) You are at a station. You are a ticket seller. Your partner wants to buy some tickets. Look at this information. Answer your partner's questions. The time now is 9 a.m.

place	price	time of next train	platform	time train arrives
Bath	single: £29.50 return: £39.70	9.15	8	10.39
Bristol	single: £36.30 return: £45.50	10.19	6	11.55

b) You want to buy these tickets. Your partner is a ticket seller. Ask your partner questions and complete the table.

ticket	price	time of next train	platform	time train arrives
two returns to Birmingham (you want to come back next weekend)				
two singles to Manchester				

Pair and Group Work: Other activities

1D ⑦ p12

a) Work with your partner. Look at the picture. Write the number of people and things.

- ...5... chairs
- .... tables
- .... men
- .... women
- .... books
- .... pens
- .... pencils
- .... apples
- .... bags
- .... mobiles

b) Work with another pair. Compare answers.

c) Check on p126. Are your answers correct?

2D ⑩ p20

a) Work with your partner. Look at the photo. Guess how old the people and dogs are. Use these ages.

girls / women		
3 6 37 41		
45 72 76		
men		
38 43 46		
65 70		
dogs		
1 8		

I think Maria is 41.

I think she's 45.

b) Check on p126. Are your answers correct?

8A ❻ p63

a) Work on your own. Think about your life when you were ten. Write six sentences about you with *was* or *were*. Use these ideas or your own.

> **When I was ten,**
> - my favourite singer / band …
> - my favourite food / drink …
> - my favourite TV programme(s) …
> - my favourite film(s) …
> - I … happy / unhappy at school.
> - I … good at (sports, languages …).
> - I … always / usually / never late for class.
> - my brother(s) / sister(s) … nice to me.

b) Work with your group. Say your sentences. Are any of the other students' sentences true for you?

> When I was ten, my favourite singer was Sting.

> Me too!

c) Tell the class two interesting things about other students in your group.

> Ali's favourite band was the Spice Girls!

9A ❾ p71

a) Work on your own. Think about the last time you visited a different town or city. Write 6–8 sentences. Use these phrases and your own ideas.

- I (go) to …
  I went to Budapest three months ago.
- I (go) there by …
- I (arrive) at … o'clock.
- I (travel) on my own / with my …
- When I was there I (visit) …
- I also (go) to …
- I (go) shopping and I (buy) …
- I (leave) there … and (get) home …
- I (be) there for … days / weeks.
- I (have) a good / great / terrible time.

b) Work on your own. Practise your sentences until you can remember them.

c) Work with your group. Tell each other about the last time you visited a different town or city.

d) Tell the class two things about the place you visited.

6D ❼ p52

a) Work on your own. Write six questions with *your favourite*. Use these ideas or your own.

> colour   actor   musician   food   drink
> restaurant   actress   band   café   singer

What's your favourite colour?
Who's your favourite actor?

b) Work with your partner. Take turns to ask your questions. Write your partner's answers.

> What's your favourite colour?

> Red.

c) Work with another student. Tell him / her about your partner in **b)**.

> Ando's favourite colour is red.

d) Tell the class two things about your first partner.

Language Summary 1

V1.1 **Numbers 0–12** (1A **7** p7)

0 zero	3 three	6 six	9 nine	11 eleven
1 one	4 four	7 seven	10 ten	12 twelve
2 two	5 five	8 eight		

V1.2 **Countries** (1B **1** p8)

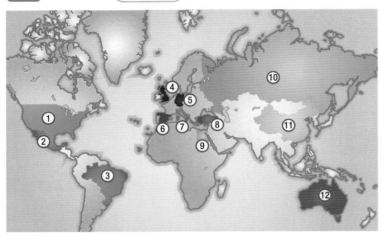

1 the USA	4 the UK	7 Italy	10 Russia
2 Mexico	5 Germany	8 Turkey	11 China
3 Brazil	6 Spain	9 Egypt	12 Australia

V1.3 **The alphabet** (1C **1** p10)

Aa Bb Cc Dd Ee Ff Gg Hh Ii Jj Kk Ll Mm
Nn Oo Pp Qq Rr Ss Tt Uu Vv Ww Xx Yy Zz

TIP! • pink letters = vowels, blue letters = consonants

V1.4 **Things in your bag (1)** (1C **6** p10)

1 a bag
2 an apple
3 a dictionary
4 a book
5 a notebook
6 a mobile
7 an iPod
8 an umbrella
9 a pencil
10 a pen

TIPS! • a mobile = a mobile phone
• UK: a mobile (phone) = US: a cell (phone)
• an iPod = an MP3 player

V1.5 **a and an** (1C **8** p11)

- We use *a* with nouns that begin with a **consonant** sound: *a bag, a dictionary, a pen*, etc.
- We use *an* with nouns that begin with a **vowel** sound: *an apple, an iPod, an umbrella*, etc.

V1.6 **People** (1D **1** p12)

a baby   a man   a woman   a boy   a girl

V1.7 **Things** (1D **2** p12)

1 a chair
2 a watch
3 a computer
4 a diary
5 a sandwich
6 a table
7 a camera

V1.8 **Plurals** (1D **4** p12)

SINGULAR	PLURAL
a chair a table a thing a boy	**+ -s** chairs tables things boys
a watch a sandwich	**+ -es** watches sandwiches
a diary a baby	**y → -ies** diaries babies
a man a woman a person	**irregular** men women people

TIP! • We also add -es to words ending in -s, -ss, -sh, -x and -z: *bus* → *buses*, *class* → *classes*, etc.

Grammar

G1.1 *I, my, you, your* 1A ❸ p6

I'm Stefan.
I'm fine, thanks.
My name's Emel.

How are **you**?
Nice to meet **you**.
What's **your** name?

TIPS! • *I / you* + **verb** (*I* **read**, *you* **listen**, etc.)
• *my / your* + **noun** (*my* **name**, *your* **book**, etc.)

G1.2 *he, his, she, her* 1B ❼ p9

What's **his** name?
His name's Stefan.
Where's **he** from?
He's from Russia.

What's **her** name?
Her name's Emel.
Where's **she** from?
She's from Turkey.

TIPS! • *he / his* = ♂, *she / her* = ♀
• *he / she* + **verb**, *his / her* + **noun**

Real World

RW1.1 **Saying hello** 1A ❶ ❷ p6

Hello, I'm Stefan.
What's your name?

Hello, my name's Emel.

Nice to meet you.

You too.

Hi, Anita.

Hi, Tim. How are you?

I'm fine, thanks. And you?

I'm OK, thanks.

RW1.2 **Introducing people** 1A ❻ p7

David, this is Polly.

Hello, Polly.
Nice to meet you.

You too.

RW1.3 **Phone numbers** 1A ❽ p7

What's your mobile number?

It's 07954 544768.

What's your home number?

It's 020 7622 3479.

TIP! • In phone numbers 0 = *oh* and 44 = *double four*.

RW1.4 **Saying goodbye** 1A ⓫ p7

Goodbye, Miki.

Bye, Lucy. See you soon.

Yes, see you.

RW1.5 **Where are you from?** 1B ❺ p8

Where are you from, Stefan?

I'm from Russia.
And you?

I'm from Turkey.

TIP! • We can say *I'm from* + city: *I'm from Moscow.*

RW1.6 **First names and surnames** 1C ❸ p10

What's your first name, please?

It's Pedro.

What's your surname?

Molina.

How do you spell that?

M–O–L–I–N–A.

RW1.7 **Classroom language** 1C ⓫ p11

Excuse me.

What does (answer) mean?

I'm sorry, I don't understand.

What's (lápiz) in English?

Can you repeat that, please?

I'm sorry, I don't know.

How do you spell (Brazil)?

TIP! • We can say *Can you repeat that, please?* or
Can you say that again, please?

Look at Classroom Instructions p127.

Language Summary 2

Vocabulary

V2.1 Nationalities 2A ❶ p14

countries	nationalities
I'm from ...	I'm ...
Italy	Italian
Brazil	Brazilian
Russia	Russian
the USA	American
Germany	German
Egypt	Egyptian
Australia	Australian
Mexico	Mexican
Turkey	Turkish
the UK	British
Spain	Spanish
China	Chinese
Japan	Japanese
France	French
Colombia	Colombian

V2.2 Jobs 2B ❶ p16

a shop assistant   an actor / an actress   a teacher

a taxi driver   a doctor   a musician

a police officer   a manager   a waiter / a waitress

TIPS! • In the Language Summaries we only show the main stress in words and phrases.
• We use *a* or *an* with jobs: *He's **a** doctor.*

V2.3 Titles 2C ❶ p18

Mr	a man (married or single)
Mrs / Ms	a married woman
Ms / Miss	a single woman

TIP! • *Mr, Mrs, Ms* or *Miss* + surname: *Mr Brown, Mrs King, Ms Roberts*, etc.

V2.4 Greetings 2C ❷ p18

Good morning, Mr Brown.
Good morning, Amanda.

Good afternoon, Mrs King.
Good afternoon.

Good evening, sir.
Good evening.

Thank you very much. Good night.
Good night, sir.

TIPS! • *Good morning, Good afternoon* and *Good evening* = *Hello*.
• *Good night* = *Goodbye*.

V2.5 Numbers 13–100 2D ❶❷❺ p20

13 thirteen	21 twenty-one	30 thirty
14 fourteen	22 twenty-two	40 forty
15 fifteen	23 twenty-three	50 fifty
16 sixteen	24 twenty-four	60 sixty
17 seventeen	25 twenty-five	70 seventy
18 eighteen	26 twenty-six	80 eighty
19 nineteen	27 twenty-seven	90 ninety
20 twenty	28 twenty-eight	100 a hundred
	29 twenty-nine	

Grammar

G2.1 *be* (singular): positive 2A ❹ p14

POSITIVE (+)

I'm (= I am)	I'm British.
you're (= you are)	You're a student.
he's (= he is)	He's Chinese.
she's (= she is)	She's Brazilian.
it's (= it is)	It's American.

TIP! • We use *it* for a thing (*a car*, *a book*, etc.).

G2.2 *be* (singular): negative 2A ❼ p15

NEGATIVE (–)

I'm not (= am not)	I'm not American.
you aren't (= are not)	You aren't a teacher.
he isn't (= is not)	He isn't from Beijing.
she isn't (= is not)	She isn't Australian.
it isn't (= is not)	It isn't a Mercedes.

TIPS! • We can also say *you're not*, *he's not*, *she's not* and *it's not*:
You're not a teacher.
He's not from Beijing.
She's not Australian.
It's not a Mercedes.
• We can't say ~~I amn't~~.

G2.3 *be* (singular): *Wh-* questions 2B ❸ p16

WH- QUESTIONS (?)

Where	am	I?	
Where	are	you	from?
Where	's	he / she / it	from?
What	's	your name?	
What	's	his / her name?	
What	's	your job?	
What	's	his / her job?	

TIPS! • *Where* = a place (*Turkey*, *London*, etc.).
• *What* = a thing (*a name*, *a job*, etc.).
• *Where's* = *Where is*, *What's* = *What is*.
• We can't write ~~Where'm I?~~ or ~~Where're you from?~~.
• We also make questions with *How*:
How are you?

G2.4 *be* (singular): *yes / no* questions and short answers 2B ❻ p17

YES / NO QUESTIONS (?)	SHORT ANSWERS
Am I in this class?	Yes, you are. No, you aren't.
Are you from Russia?	Yes, I am. No, I'm not.
Is he a doctor?	Yes, he is. No, he isn't.
Is she Italian?	Yes, she is. No, she isn't.
Is it Japanese?	Yes, it is. No, it isn't.

TIPS! • We can also say: *No, you're not*. *No, he's not*. *No, she's not*. and *No, it's not*.
• We can't say ~~Yes, you're.~~, ~~Yes, I'm.~~, ~~Yes, he's.~~, ~~Yes, she's.~~ or ~~Yes, it's.~~

Real World

RW2.1 Email addresses 2C ❸ p18

.	dot
@	at
-	hyphen /'haɪfən/
_	underscore
A	capital a

To: eve.smith@webmail.com

eve **dot** smith **at** webmail **dot** com

RW2.2 Personal information questions 2C ❼ p19

What's your first name, please?
What's your surname?
Are you married?
What's your nationality?
What's your address?
What's your mobile number?
What's your email address?

RW2.3 *How old ... ?* 2D ❽ p20

How old is your house? — It's a hundred years old.

How old are you? — I'm thirty.

TIPS! • We don't usually say *years old* for people:
I'm thirty., *Emily's nine.*, etc.
• We say *I'm thirty.* not ~~I have thirty.~~ or ~~I'm thirty years.~~

Language Summary 3

V3.1 Adjectives (1) 3A ❶ p22

friendly   unfriendly   beautiful   ugly

big   small   good   bad

hot   cold   expensive   cheap

new   old   nice

V3.2 Word order with adjectives; *very* 3A ❷ p22

- **Adjectives** go after *be*: *Your watch is nice.*
- **Adjectives** go before **nouns**: *It's a new car.*
- **Adjectives** are not plural with **plural nouns**: *They're good friends.* not *They're goods friends.*
- We put **very** before **adjectives**: *It's very hot.*

It's hot.   It's very hot.

TIP! • Notice the word order in questions: **Are** *you cold?*, **Is** *he friendly?*, **Is** *the camera expensive?*, etc.

V3.3 Family 3B ❷ p24 ❼ p25

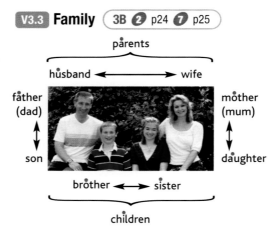

parents
husband ⟷ wife
father (dad)   mother (mum)
son   daughter
brother ⟷ sister
children

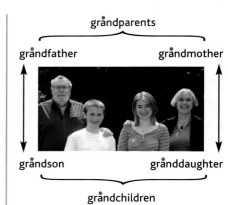

grandparents
grandfather   grandmother
grandson   granddaughter
grandchildren

TIPS! • The plural of *wife* is *wives* not *wifes*.
• The singular of *children* is *child*.

TIP! • The singular of *grandchildren* is *grandchild*.

V3.4 Food and drink (1) 3C ❻ p26

a coffee   a cappuccino   an espresso   a tea   a mineral water

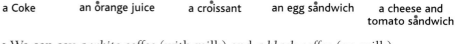

a Coke   an orange juice   a croissant   an egg sandwich   a cheese and tomato sandwich

TIP! • We can say *a white coffee* (with milk) and *a black coffee* (no milk).

V3.5 Food and drink (2)
3D ❶ p28

1	fruit	9	fish
2	tea	10	rice
3	coffee	11	meat
4	vegetables	12	cheese
5	orange juice	13	eggs
6	milk	14	sugar
7	bread	15	pasta
8	water	16	chocolate

V3.6 *love, like, eat, drink, a lot of* 3D ❸ p28

I love chocolate.   I like fish.   I eat a lot of rice.   I drink a lot of coffee.

Grammar

G3.1 *be* (plural): positive and negative
(3A ⑥ p23)

POSITIVE (+)

we're (= we are)	We're in a new hotel.
you're (= you are)	You're from the UK.
they're (= they are)	They're very big.

NEGATIVE (–)

we aren't (= are not)	We aren't in the hotel now.
you aren't	You aren't from Russia.
they aren't	They aren't very expensive.

TIPS! • *You* is singular and plural:
You're a student. You're students.
• We use *they* for people or things.
• We can also say *we're not, you're not* and
they're not.

G3.2 *be* (plural): questions and short

 answers (3A ⑪ p23)

WH- QUESTIONS (?)

Where	are	we?
Where	are	you?
Where	are	they?
Where	are	Fiona and Nick?

YES / NO QUESTIONS (?)	SHORT ANSWERS
Are we in room A?	Yes, you are. No, you aren't.
Are you in London?	Yes, we are. No, we aren't.
Are they in a small hotel?	Yes, they are. No, they aren't.

TIP! • We can also say: *No, we're not.*
No, you're not. and *No, they're not.*

G3.3 Possessive *'s* (3B ④ p24)

• We use a name (*Nick*, etc.) or a noun for a
person (*sister*, etc.) + *'s* for the possessive.
Fiona is Nick's wife.
It's my sister's car.

TIPS! • *'s* can mean *is* or **the possessive**:
She's my sister. ('s = is)
Kevin is Nick's son. ('s = possessive)
• We can also use *'s* with other nouns for
people: *It's my **teacher's** car. He's the **doctor's**
son. It's his **friend's** camera.*, etc.
• For plural nouns, we write *s'*:
It's my parents' house. He's my friends' son.

G3.4 Subject pronouns (*I, you*, etc.) and possessive adjectives
(*my, your*, etc.) (3B ⑨ p25)

subject pronouns	I	you	he	she	it	we	they
possessive adjectives	my	your	his	her	its	our	their

• We use **subject pronouns** with verbs: *I'm, you listen, they read*, etc.
• We use **possessive adjectives** with nouns: *my sister, your family, his dog*, etc.
*I'm Mary and this is Sid, **my** husband.*
***Her** husband's name is Nick and **he's** a doctor.*
*These are **their** two children – **our** grandchildren.*
***It's** a very nice photo, I think.*

Real World

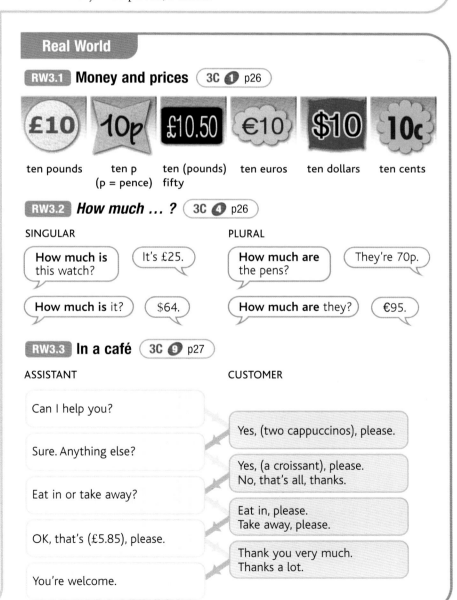

RW3.1 Money and prices (3C ① p26)

£10	10p	£10.50	€10	$10	10c
ten pounds	ten p (p = pence)	ten (pounds) fifty	ten euros	ten dollars	ten cents

RW3.2 *How much ... ?* (3C ④ p26)

SINGULAR

How much is this watch? — It's £25.

How much is it? — $64.

PLURAL

How much are the pens? — They're 70p.

How much are they? — €95.

RW3.3 In a café (3C ⑨ p27)

ASSISTANT

Can I help you?

Sure. Anything else?

Eat in or take away?

OK, that's (£5.85), please.

You're welcome.

CUSTOMER

Yes, (two cappuccinos), please.

Yes, (a croissant), please.
No, that's all, thanks.

Eat in, please.
Take away, please.

Thank you very much.
Thanks a lot.

Language Summary 4

V4.1 Phrases with *like, have, live, work, study* (4A ➊ p30)

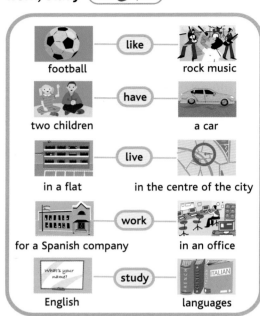

like — football / rock music
have — two children / a car
live — in a flat / in the centre of the city
work — for a Spanish company / in an office
study — English / languages

V4.2 Free time activities (4B ➊ p32)

watch TV or DVDs   go shopping

go to the cinema   go out with friends

eat out   play tennis

go to concerts   play computer games

TIP! • We can say *I watch TV **a lot**.*, etc.

V4.3 Things to buy (4C ➊ p34)

a magazine   tissues   a map   a newspaper   a postcard

a birthday card   batteries   chewing gum   sweets   a box of chocolates

TIP! • The plural of *box* is *boxes*. The singular of *batteries* is *a battery*.

V4.4 *this, that, these, those* (4C ➌ p34 ➎ p35)

	here ↓	there ↗
singular	this	that
plural	these	those

Are these your postcards?   That's my car!   What are those?   Is this your newspaper?

TIPS! • *This, that, these, those* go <u>before</u> *be* in sentences: *Those are nice.*
• *This, that, these, those* go <u>after</u> *be* in questions: *How much are these?*

V4.5 Days of the week (4D ➊ p36)

Monday Tuesday Wednesday Thursday Friday Saturday Sunday

TIP! • Saturday and Sunday = *the weekend*

V4.6 Time words (4D ➋ p36)

60 **seconds** = 1 **minute**
60 minutes = 1 **hour**
24 hours = 1 **day**
7 days = 1 **week**
365 days = 1 **year**
12 **months** = 1 year

TIPS! • 30 minutes = half an hour
• 15 minutes = quarter of an hour
• 18 months = a year and a half
• We say *two and a half years* not ~~two years and a half~~.

Grammar

G4.1 **Present Simple (*I, you, we, they*): positive and negative** **4A ❸** p31

POSITIVE (+)

I **work** for a car company.
You **study** English.
We **live** in a very nice flat.
They **like** football.

TIP! • The Present Simple positive is the same for *I, you, we* and *they*.

NEGATIVE (–)

I	don't	have	a new car.	(don't = do not)
You	don't	study	German.	
We	don't	have	a daughter.	
They	don't	like	homework.	

TIP! • The Present Simple negative is the same for *I, you, we* and *they*.

G4.2 **Present Simple (*I, you, we, they*): questions and short answers** **4B ❹** p32

WH- QUESTIONS (?)

Where	do	you	live	in the UK?
What music	do	you	like?	
What	do	you	do	in your free time?
What food	do	you	like?	

TIPS! • Present Simple questions are the same for *I, you, we* and *they*.

• We can say *What do you do?* to ask about a person's job:

A *What do you do?*
B *I'm a doctor.*

YES / NO QUESTIONS (?)	SHORT ANSWERS
Do I **know** you?	Yes, you do. No, you don't.
Do you **like** London?	Yes, I do. No, I don't.
Do we **have** a class today?	Yes, you do. No, you don't.
Do you **go** to concerts?	Yes, we do. No, we don't.
Do they **like** Mexican food?	Yes, they do. No, they don't.

TIP! • We don't use *like, have*, etc. in short answers:

A *Do you like London?*
B *Yes, I do.* not ~~Yes, I like~~ or ~~Yes, I do like.~~

Real World

RW4.1 **In a shop** **4C ❼** p35

CUSTOMER — SHOP ASSISTANT

Excuse me. Do you have any (maps of London)?
→ Yes, they're over there.

How much is (this map)?
→ It's (£4.75).

How much are (these postcards)?
→ They're (50p) each.

Can I have (that box of chocolates), please?
→ Sure. Anything else?

Yes, this (birthday card), please.
No, that's all, thanks.
→ OK, that's (£10.65).

Here you are.
→ Thanks a lot.
Thanks very much.

RW4.2 **Telling the time** **4D ❸❹** p36

six o'clock / six   five past six   ten past six   quarter past six / six fifteen

twenty past six   twenty-five past six   half past six / six thirty   twenty-five to seven

twenty to seven   quarter to seven / six forty-five   ten to seven   five to seven

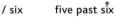

TIPS! • We can say *quarter past / to ...* or *a quarter past / to ...* .

• We can also say the time like this: *six twenty, six fifty-five*, etc.

• UK: *five past six* = US: *five after six*

RW4.3 **Talking about the time** **4D ❼** p36

What time is it, please?
It's twenty to three.

What time is your English class?
It's at half past eight.

TIPS! • We can say *What time is it?* or *What's the time?*.

• We use *at* for times: *My class is **at** four o'clock.*

• a.m. = 0.00–12.00, p.m. = 12.00–24.00

Language Summary 5

V5.1 Daily routines (5A **1** p38)

| get up | have breakfast | leave home |

start work   have lunch   finish work

get home   have dinner   go to bed   sleep

V5.2 Time phrases with *on, in, at*
(5B **1** p40)

on	in	at
Sunday	the morning	six o'clock
Monday	the afternoon	half past ten
Tuesday morning	the evening	midday
Friday afternoon	the week	midnight
Saturday evening		night
		the weekend

TIPS! • We say *in the morning / afternoon / evening*, but *at night* not ~~in the night~~.
• *midday* = 12.00, *midnight* = 24.00

V5.3 Food and drink (3)

chicken salad   vegetable lasagne   burger and chips   mushroom pizza   apple pie and cream

fruit salad   chocolate ice cream   strawberry ice cream   vanilla ice cream   a bottle of still mineral water

a bottle of sparkling mineral water   a Coke   an orange juice   a coffee   a tea

V5.4 Frequency adverbs and phrases with *every* (5D **1 4** p44)

FREQUENCY ADVERBS

always	usually	sometimes	not usually	never

100%   0%

PHRASES WITH *EVERY*

• We can use ***every* + time word**: *every day, every week, every month, every year*, etc.

TIPS! • We say *every day* not ~~every days~~, *every week* not ~~every weeks~~, etc.
• We can also say *every morning, every afternoon, every evening, every night, every Monday, every Friday evening, every six weeks, every four years*, etc.

WORD ORDER

• **Frequency adverbs** go after ***be***: *I'm **always** tired on Sundays. It's **not usually** very busy.*

• **Frequency adverbs** go before other **verbs**: *I **never** have breakfast. I don't **usually** go out.*

• **Phrases with *every*** are usually at the end of the sentence: *I work **every Saturday**. I play football **every Sunday morning***

TIP! • We can say *I'm always tired on **Sunday**.* or *I'm always tired on **Sundays**.*

Grammar

G5.1 Present Simple (*he, she, it*): positive and negative
5A ❹ p39

POSITIVE (+)

● In positive sentences with *he, she* and *it* we add **-s** or **-es** to the verb: *She start**s** work at nine o'clock. He watch**es** TV in the evening. It finish**es** at midnight.*

spelling rule	examples
most verbs: add **-s**	like**s** leave**s** work**s** get**s** sleep**s**
verbs ending in *-ch* or *-sh*: add **-es**	watch**es** teach**es** finish**es**
verbs ending in consonant + *y*: *y* → **-ies**	stud**ies**
the verbs *go* and *do*: add **-es**	goe**s** doe**s**
the verb *have* is irregular	**has**

NEGATIVE (−)

He	doesn't	have	a car.
She	doesn't	like	mornings.
She	doesn't	watch	TV after dinner.
It	doesn't	start	today.

(doesn't = does not)

TIP! ● The negative is the same for *he, she* and *it*: **He** *doesn't have a car.* **It** *doesn't start today.*

G5.2 Present Simple (*he, she, it*): questions and short answers
5B ❹ p41

WH- QUESTIONS (?)

Where	does	Nadine	work	at the weekend?
What	does	she	do	in the week?
Where	does	she	live	in Manchester?
What	does	she	do	in her free time?
What time	does	he	get up	on Sunday?
When	does	it	start?	

TIP! ● Present Simple questions are the same for *he, she* and *it*.

YES / NO QUESTIONS (?)	SHORT ANSWERS
Does he know Nadine?	Yes, he does. No, he doesn't.
Does she like Manchester?	Yes, she does. No, she doesn't.
Does it start at 7.30?	Yes, it does. No, it doesn't.

● We use **does** in questions with *he, she* and *it*.
● We use **do** in questions with *I, you, we* and *they*.

TIPS! ● We say *Does she work at home?* not ~~Does she works at home?~~.
● We don't use *like, have*, etc. in short answers: A *Does he like fish?* B *Yes, he does.* not ~~Yes, he likes.~~ or ~~Yes, he does like.~~

Real World

RW5.1 In a restaurant
5C ❹ p43

WAITER — CUSTOMERS

Are you ready to order?

Yes. Can I have (the chicken salad), please? And can I have (the vegetable lasagne)?

Certainly.

What would you like to drink?

(A Coke) for me, please. And can we have (a bottle of mineral water)?

Still or sparkling?

Sparkling, please.

OK. Thanks very much.

Would you like a dessert?

Not for me, thanks. (The apple pie) for me. And (two coffees), please.

Certainly.

Excuse me. Can we have the bill, please?

Of course.

Thanks a lot.

TIP! ● We can use *the* or *a* when we order food: *Can I have **the / a** chicken salad, please?*

Language Summary 6

V6.1 Places in a town or city (1) 6A 1 p46

a park | a station | a theatre

a building | a river | an airport

a bus station | a museum | a shopping centre

TIP! • a station = a train station

V6.2 Places in a town or city (2) 6B 1 p48

a bank | a chemist's | a road

a cashpoint / an ATM | a bus stop | a supermarket

a square | a market | a post office

V6.3 Things in your bag (2) 6C 1 p50

1 a map
2 a purse
3 a camera
4 keys
5 a laptop
6 a passport
7 a guide book
8 a wallet
9 an ID card
10 a credit card
11 money

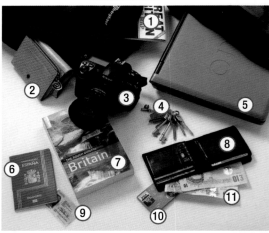

V6.4 Clothes 6D 1 p52

1 a shirt	4 trousers	7 boots	10 jeans	13 a coat
2 a tie	5 a jumper	8 a jacket	11 trainers	14 shoes
3 a suit	6 a skirt	9 a T-shirt	12 a dress	

TIPS! • We can say **a pair of** trousers / jeans / shoes / trainers / boots.

• Clothes /kləʊðz/ is always plural: Your clothes **are** over there.

V6.5 Colours 6D 2 p52

black **white** **yellow** **brown** **red** **blue** **grey** **pink** **green**

TIP! • We use What colour's / are … ? to ask about colours:
What colour's Wayne's tie? **What colour are** Lisa's shoes?

V6.6 *favourite* (6D 6 p52)

- *favourite* = the thing or person we like best.

My **favourite** colour is pink.

This is my **favourite** jacket.

These are my **favourite** boots.

What's your **favourite** colour?

Who's your **favourite** actor?

TIP! • We use *Who* to ask about a person:
A **Who**'s your favourite actor?
B *Brad Pitt.*

My favourite colour is pink!

Grammar

G6.1 *a, some, a lot of*; *there is / there are*: positive
(6A 4 p47)

A, SOME, A LOT OF

There's **a person** in the park. / There are **some people** in the park. / There are **a lot of people** in the park.

- We use *a* or *an* with singular nouns: *a person*, *an airport*, etc.
- We use *some* and *a lot of* with plural nouns: *some museums*, *a lot of restaurants*, etc.

TIP! • We can say *a lot of* or *lots of*: There are **lots of** people in the park.

THERE IS / THERE ARE: POSITIVE
singular
There's a big new shopping centre. (**there's** = there is)
There's an airport in Bristol.

plural
There are five theatres.
There are some very nice parks.
There are a lot of old buildings.

TIP! • We write *there are* not ~~there're~~.

Real World

RW6.1 At the tourist information centre (6C 4 p51)

TOURIST | ASSISTANT

Good morning.
— Hello. Can I help you?
Yes, please.

Do you have a (map of the city centre)?
— Yes, of course. Here you are.
Thank you. How much is it?
— It's (a pound).

When is the (Roman Baths Museum) open?
— It's open from (nine) a.m. to (five) p.m.
Is it closed on (Mondays)?
— No, it's open every day.

Where's the (Thermae Bath Spa)?
— It's in (Hot Bath Street).
Can you show me on this map?
— Yes, of course. Here it is. It's about (five) minutes away.
Thank you very much.

G6.2 *there is / there are*: negative, *yes / no* questions and short answers; *any* (6B 3 p49)

NEGATIVE (–)
There isn't a station near here.
There aren't any good restaurants near here.

YES / NO QUESTIONS (?)	SHORT ANSWERS
Is there a bank?	Yes, there is. No, there isn't.
Are there any shops?	Yes, there are. No, there aren't.

TIP! • We say *Yes, there is.* not ~~Yes, there's.~~

ANY

- We use *any* in negatives and questions with *there are*:
There aren't **any** *good restaurants near here.*
Are there **any** *shops?*

TIP! • We use *some* in positive sentences with *there are*:
There are **some** *very nice restaurants in the centre.*

111

Language Summary 7

V7.1 Things you like and don't like (7A ❶ p54)

animals

classical music

visiting new places

horror films

watching sport on TV

shopping for clothes

soap operas

dancing

flying

TIPS! • UK: *film* = US: *movie*
• *TV* = *television*

V7.2 love, like, hate (7A ❸ p54)

I love ...

I like ...

I don't like ...

I hate ...

• After *like, love* and *hate* we can use a **noun** or **verb+ing**.
I love **animals**.
I like **soap operas**.
I don't like **dancing**.
I hate **shopping** for clothes.

SPELLING OF VERB+ING FORMS

• Most verbs: *visit* → *visit**ing***, *watch* → *watch**ing***,
fly → *fly**ing***, etc.
• Verbs ending in *-e: dance* → *danc**ing*** (not ~~danceing~~), etc.
• Verbs ending in consonant + vowel + consonant:
shop → *shop**ping*** (not ~~shoping~~), etc.

TIP! • We don't use *the* when we talk about things we like
or don't like in general: *I love dogs.* (= all dogs), *I don't like
sport.* (= all sport).

V7.3 Abilities (7B ❶ p56)

ski

ride a bike

drive

swim

speak German

play the piano

sing

play the guitar

play basketball

cook

TIPS! • We say *play basketball /
football / tennis* but *play **the** piano /
the guitar*.
• *a bike = a bicycle*

V7.4 Prepositions of place (7C ❷ p58)

The café is **on** the left.

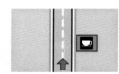
The café is **on** the right.

The café is **in** King Street.

The café is **opposite** the bank.

The café is **next to** the bank.

The café is **near** the bank.

TIP! • We can say **in** *King Street* or **on** *King Street*.

Grammar

G7.1 Object pronouns (7A ❼ p55)

- Look at these sentences. Notice the word order.
  Subject pronouns go **before** the verb.
  Object pronouns go **after** the verb.

subject	verb	object
I	love	soap operas.
Jack	hates	them.

subject pronouns	I	you	he	she	it	we	they
object pronouns	me	you	him	her	it	us	them

V7.5 Things people do online (7D ❶ p60)

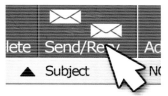

send and receive emails

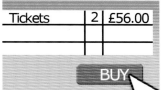

buy concert or theatre tickets

watch videos or TV programmes

listen to the radio

chat to friends or family

buy and sell things

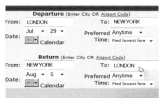

book flights or holidays

download music

TIPS! • We say *receive emails* or *get emails*: *I **get** lots of emails every day*.

• *online* = connected to the Internet: *Do you chat to friends **online**?*

G7.2 *can*: positive and negative (7B ❸ p56)

- We use *can* or *can't* to talk about ability.
- *Can* and *can't* are the same for *I, you, he, she, it, we* and *they*.

POSITIVE (+)

She	can	play	the piano.
They	can	ski.	

NEGATIVE (–)

I	can't	swim.	
We	can't	speak	Chinese.

TIPS! • We sometimes use *(very) well* with *can*: *They can ski **(very) well***.

• We say *She **can play** the piano*. not *She ~~can to play the piano~~*.

G7.3 *can*: *yes / no* questions and short answers (7B ❽ p57)

YES / NO QUESTIONS (?)	SHORT ANSWERS
Can you cook?	Yes, I can.
Can you play the piano?	No, I can't.
Can he play the guitar?	Yes, he can.
Can she speak German?	No, she can't.
Can they swim?	Yes, they can.
Can they play basketball?	No, they can't.

TIP! • We don't use *do* or *does* in questions with *can*: **Can you** cook? not ~~Do you can cook?~~.

Real World

RW7.1 Asking for and giving directions (7C ❻ p59)

ASKING FOR DIRECTIONS

Excuse me. Where's the (museum)?

Excuse me. Is there a (bank) near here?

GIVING DIRECTIONS

Go along this road and turn left.

Go along this road and turn right.

That's (Park Street).

The (museum) is on the right, next to the (theatre).

The (bank) is on the left, opposite the (station).

It's over there, near the (cinema).

TIP! • We can say *on **the** right / left* or *on **your** right / left*.

Language Summary 8

V8.1 Adjectives (2) (8A ❶ p62)

   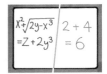

short   long   terrible   great   right   wrong   difficult   easy
                 awful   fantastic
                       amazing

interesting   boring   happy   unhappy   old   young   full   empty

V8.2 Years and past time phrases (8B ❶ ❷ p64)

YEARS

1887 = eighteen eighty-seven

1900 = nineteen hundred

1980 = nineteen eighty

2000 = two thousand

2009 = two thousand and nine

2010 = twenty ten

TIPS! • For the years 2000–2009, we usually say *two thousand, two thousand and one*, etc.

• For the years 2010–2099, we usually say *twenty ten, twenty eleven*, etc.

• We use *in* with years: ***in** 1980, **in** 2009*, etc.

PAST TIME PHRASES

Joe was in Paris **last** week.

He was at home **yesterday** afternoon.

He was in bed four hours **ago**.

He's at work **now**.

TIPS! • We use *last* with days (*last Monday*) and months (*last June*).

• We also say *last night, last week, last weekend, last month, last year*.

• We say *yesterday morning, yesterday afternoon* and *yesterday evening*, but *last night* not ~~yesterday night~~.

• *four hours **ago*** = four hours before now

V8.3 Months and dates (8C ❶ ❷ p66)

MONTHS

January	May	September
February	June	October
March	July	November
April	August	December

TIPS! • We use capital letters with months.

• We use *in* with months: ***in** January, **in** May*, etc.

DATES

1st	first	16th	sixteenth
2nd	second	17th	seventeenth
3rd	third	18th	eighteenth
4th	fourth	19th	nineteenth
5th	fifth	20th	twentieth
6th	sixth	21st	twenty-first
7th	seventh	22nd	twenty-second
8th	eighth	23rd	twenty-third
9th	ninth	24th	twenty-fourth
10th	tenth	25th	twenty-fifth
11th	eleventh	26th	twenty-sixth
12th	twelfth	27th	twenty-seventh
13th	thirteenth	28th	twenty-eighth
14th	fourteenth	29th	twenty-ninth
15th	fifteenth	30th	thirtieth
		31st	thirty-first

V8.4 Big numbers (8D ❶ p68)

150 = a hundred and fifty

390 = three hundred and ninety

1,000 = a thousand

16,200 = sixteen thousand, two hundred

750,000 = seven hundred and fifty thousand

1,000,000 = a million

50,000,000 = fifty million

TIPS! • We don't use a plural -s with *hundred, thousand* or *million*: *three hundred* not ~~three hundreds~~, etc.

• We use *and* after *hundred*, but not after *thousand*: *a hundred **and** fifty*, but *sixteen thousand, two hundred*.

• We can say ***a** hundred* or ***one** hundred, **a** thousand* or ***one** thousand* and ***a** million* or ***one** million*.

Grammar

G8.1 **Past Simple of _be_: positive and negative**
(8A **3** p63)

POSITIVE (+)	NEGATIVE (−)
I **was**	I **wasn't** (= was not)
you **were**	you **weren't** (= were not)
he / she / it **was**	he / she / it **wasn't**
we **were**	we **weren't**
they **were**	they **weren't**

I **was** at the World Cup Final.
We **were** near the Opera House.
The stadium **wasn't** full.
They **weren't** very happy.

TIP! • The past of _there is / there are_ is _there was / there were_:
There was a big party. **There were** some amazing fireworks.

G8.2 **Past Simple of _be_: questions and short answers; _was born / were born_** (8B **5** p65)

_WH-_ QUESTIONS (?)

Where	was	I / he / she / it last week?
When	were	you / we / they in Australia?

Where	was	the wedding?
How old	were	Rajeet and Gita?
How many people	were	at the wedding?
Where	was	Rajeet's brother?

YES / NO QUESTIONS (?)	SHORT ANSWERS
Was I / he / she / it at the wedding?	Yes, I / he / she / it **was**. No, I / he / she / it **wasn't**.
Were you / we / they at the wedding?	Yes, you / we / they **were**. No, you / we / they **weren't**.

TIP! • We can also make questions with _there was / there were_: **Was there** a party? **Were there** a lot of people?

WAS BORN / WERE BORN

(Where was Gita born?)

((She was born) in the UK.)

(When were you born?)

((I was born) in 1987.)

TIP! • We say _I was born in Rome._ not ~~I borned in Rome.~~

Real World

RW8.1 **Talking about days and dates** (8C **3** p66)

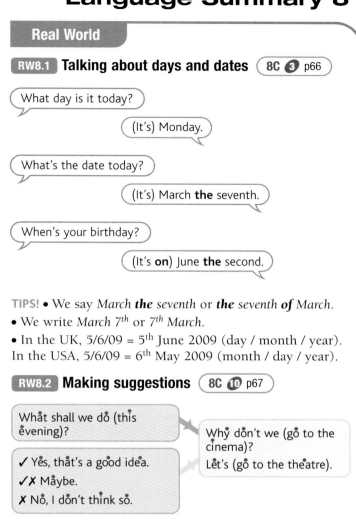

(What day is it today?)

((It's) Monday.)

(What's the date today?)

((It's) March **the** seventh.)

(When's your birthday?)

((It's **on**) June **the** second.)

TIPS! • We say _March **the** seventh_ or _**the** seventh **of** March_.
• We write _March 7ᵗʰ_ or _7ᵗʰ March_.
• In the UK, 5/6/09 = 5ᵗʰ June 2009 (day / month / year).
In the USA, 5/6/09 = 6ᵗʰ May 2009 (month / day / year).

RW8.2 **Making suggestions** (8C **10** p67)

(What shall we do (this evening)?)

(Why don't we (go to the cinema)? Let's (go to the theatre).)

(✓ Yes, that's a good idea. ✓✗ Maybe. ✗ No, I don't think so.)

(Where shall we meet?)

(Let's meet at (the theatre).)

(What time shall we meet?)

(About seven o'clock.)

Language Summary 9

V9.1 Transport 9A ❶ p70

a car

a bus

a train

a taxi

a bike

a motorbike

a plane

a boat

TIPS! • UK: *a taxi* = US: *a cab*
• We say *I go / come / travel* **by** *car, bus,* etc.:
I usually go to work **by** *car.*
• We also say: *I* **walk** *to work / school,* etc.
• *go by plane = fly, go by car = drive,*
go by bike = cycle.

V9.2 Holiday activities 9B ❶ p72

Match these phrases to pictures a)–k).

1 [e] go on holiday
2 [ ] take photos
3 [ ] go to the beach
4 [ ] stay with friends
     or family
5 [ ] stay in a hotel
6 [ ] go sightseeing
7 [ ] go swimming
8 [ ] go for a walk
9 [ ] rent a car
10 [ ] travel around
11 [ ] have a good time

TIP! • UK: *go on holiday* =
US: *go on vacation*

V9.3 At the station 9C ❹ p75

a customer   a ticket office

a ticket machine

a platform

a single

a return

TIP! • *a single* = a single ticket, *a return* = a return ticket

V9.4 Question words 9D ❷ p76

QUESTION WORD	ASKS ABOUT ...	EXAMPLE
Who	a person	**Who**'s she?
What	a thing	**What**'s that?
When	a time	**When** do you start work?
Where	a place	**Where** does he live?
Why	a reason	**Why** are you tired?
How old	age	**How old** are they?
How many	a number	**How many** people are there?
How much	an amount of money	**How much** are those shoes?

TIPS! • We also use *What time … ?* to ask about a time:
A **What time** do you go to bed? B *At half past eleven.*
• We usually answer *Why … ?* questions with *Because … :*
A *Why are you tired?* B **Because** *I got up at 5 a.m.*

(a)

(b)

(c)

(d)

(e)

(f)

(g)

(h)

(i)

(j)

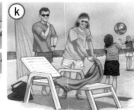
(k)

Grammar

G9.1 Past Simple: positive (regular and irregular verbs) 9A ⑤ p71

REGULAR VERBS

- To make the Past Simple of regular verbs, we usually add -ed to the verb: want**ed**, start**ed**, visit**ed**, etc.
- For regular verbs ending in -e (like, arrive, etc.), we add -d to the verb: like**d**, arrive**d**, etc.

TIPS! • The Past Simple of travel is travel**led**.

• The Past Simple of study is stud**ied**.

REGULAR VERBS IN UNITS 1–10

arrive	like	practise	turn
ask	listen	receive	use
check	live	rent	visit
cook	look	repeat	walk
finish	love	show	want
hate	move	start	watch
help	play	stay	work

IRREGULAR VERBS

- Many verbs in English are irregular. There are no spelling rules for irregular verbs.

IRREGULAR VERBS IN UNITS 1–10

verb	Past Simple	verb	Past Simple
buy	bought	put	put
choose	chose	read /riːd/	read /red/
come	came	ride	rode
do	did	say	said /sed/
drink	drank	see	saw /sɔː/
drive	drove	sell	sold
eat	ate	send	sent
feel	felt	sing	sang
find	found	sleep	slept
fly	flew	speak	spoke
get	got	spend	spent
give	gave	swim	swam
go	went	take	took
have	had	teach	taught /tɔːt/
hear	heard /hɜːd/	tell	told
know	knew	think	thought /θɔːt/
leave	left	understand	understood
make	made	wear	wore
meet	met	write	wrote

TIPS! • The Past Simple of regular and irregular verbs is the same for I, you, he, she, it, we and they.

• The Past Simple of be is was or were (see G8.1).

G9.2 Past Simple: negative 9B ④ p72

I	didn't	stay	in a hotel.
She	didn't	visit	any other places.
He	didn't	go	swimming.
We	didn't	go	on holiday last year.

(didn't = did not)

TIPS! • We say I / you / he / she / it / we / they **didn't** … .

• The Past Simple negative of be is wasn't or weren't (see G8.1).

G9.3 Past Simple: questions and short answers 9B ⑧ p73

WH- QUESTIONS (?)

Where	did	Nancy	go	on holiday?
Who	did	she	stay	with?
When	did	he	go	to the beach?
How many photos	did	they	take?	

YES / NO QUESTIONS (?)	SHORT ANSWERS
Did he go swimming?	Yes, he did. / No, he didn't.
Did they visit China last year?	Yes, they did. / No, they didn't.

TIPS! • We say **Did** I / you / he / she / it / we / they … ?

• We don't use did in questions with was and were (see G8.2).

• Notice the difference between negatives and questions in the Present Simple and Past Simple:

PRESENT SIMPLE	PAST SIMPLE
I **don't** live in a flat.	I **didn't** live in a flat.
He **doesn't** have a car.	He **didn't** have a car.
Where **do** you work?	Where **did** you work?
Where **does** she live?	Where **did** she live?

Real World

RW9.1 Buying train tickets 9C ⑤ p75

CUSTOMER	TICKET SELLER
(Two returns) to (Liverpool), please.	When do you want to come back?
(Tomorrow evening).	OK. That's (ninety-three pounds forty), please. Here are your tickets.
Thanks. What time's the next train?	There's one at (nine seventeen).
Which platform?	Platform (six).
What time does it arrive in (Liverpool)?	At (twelve twenty-nine).
Thanks a lot. Bye.	

Language Summary 10

V10.1 Future plans (10A **1** p78)

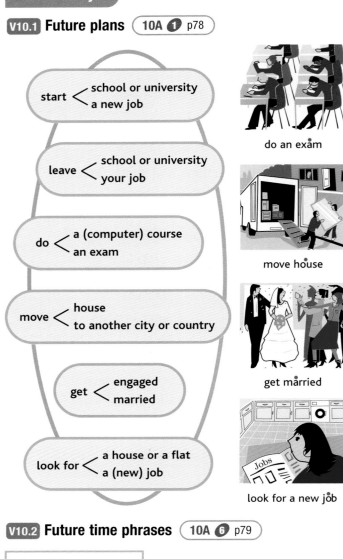

start < school or university / a new job

leave < school or university / your job

do < a (computer) course / an exam

move < house / to another city or country

get < engaged / married

look for < a house or a flat / a (new) job

do an exam

move house

get married

look for a new job

V10.2 Future time phrases (10A **6** p79)

tonight
tomorrow morning
next week
next month
in December
in 2025

TIPS! • We say *tonight* not ~~this night~~.
• We can say *tomorrow morning, tomorrow afternoon, tomorrow evening* and *tomorrow night*.
• We use *next* in these phrases: *next week, next weekend, next month, next year*.
• We use *in* with months (*in December*) and years (*in 2025*).
• We can also use *next* with months (*next June*) and days (*next Monday*).
• We also use *on* with days (*on Monday*).

V10.3 Phrases with *have, watch, go, go to* (10B **1** p80)

have
dinner with friends
coffee with friends
a party

have a party

watch
TV
the news
sport on TV

watch the news

go
shopping
swimming
running

go running

go to
the cinema
the gym
a party

go to the gym

V10.4 Adjectives (3): feelings (10C **1** p82)

happy   sad   excited

angry   bored

hungry   tired   scared

TIP! • We can say *I'm* excited, etc. or *I **feel** excited*, etc.

Grammar

G10.1 *be going to*: positive and negative (10A **3** p79)

- We use *be going to* + verb to talk about future plans.

POSITIVE (+)

I	'm	going to	do	a computer course.
He / She	's	going to	leave	his / her job.
We / You / They	're	going to	travel	around the UK.

NEGATIVE (−)

I	'm not	going to	start	university this year.
He / She	isn't	going to	work	in London.
We / You / They	aren't	going to	stay	here.

TIP! • With the verb *go* we usually say: *I'm going to the cinema.* not *I'm going to go to the cinema.* But both sentences are correct.

G10.2 *be going to*: questions and short answers (10B **4** p80)

WH- QUESTIONS (?)

What	am	I		going to	do	tomorrow?
Where	are	you / we / they		going to	live?	
When	's (is)	he / she		going to	move	to Australia?

YES / NO QUESTIONS (?)	SHORT ANSWERS
Are you going to **watch** a film?	Yes, I am. No, I'm not.
Is he / she going to **look for** a job?	Yes, he / she is. No, he / she isn't.
Are you going to **sell** your flat?	Yes, we are. No, we aren't.
Are they going to **have** a party?	Yes, they are. No, they aren't.

Real World

RW10.1 Saying goodbye and good luck (10C **4** p83)

Have a good holiday! — Thanks a lot.

See you in September. — Yes, see you.

Good luck with your exam. — Thanks very much.

Have a good	holiday! journey! day! weekend! birthday! time!	See you	in (September). in (two weeks). next (month). on (Monday).	Good luck with your	exam. new job. English test. new school.

Recording Scripts

R1.4

A

SUE Hello, my name's Sue. What's your name?

MARIO Hello, I'm Mario.

S Nice to meet you.

M You too.

B

ADAM Hi, Meg.

MEG Hi, Adam. How are you?

A I'm fine, thanks. And you?

M I'm OK, thanks.

R1.8

A

A What's your home number?

B It's 020 7599 6320.

A 020 7599 6320.

B Yes, that's right.

B

A What's your mobile number?

B It's 07655 421769.

A 07655 421769.

B Yes, that's right.

A Thanks.

C

A What's your phone number in Madrid?

B It's 00 34 91 532 67 53.

A 00 34 91 …

B … 532 67 53.

A OK. Thank you.

R1.11

EMEL Where are you from, Stefan?

STEFAN I'm from Russia. And you?

E I'm from Turkey.

R1.12

Where are you from? | I'm from Russia. | And you? | I'm from Turkey.

R1.13

ANSWERS 2a) 3d) 4c)

R1.14

1 Her name's Juliette Binoche. She's from France. 2 His name's Daniel Craig. He's from the UK. 3 Her name's Nicole Kidman. She's from Australia. 4 His name's Will Smith. He's from the USA. 5 Her name's Penélope Cruz. She's from Spain. 6 His name's Jackie Chan. He's from China.

R1.16

1 u v 2 y i 3 g j 4 b v 5 a r 6 e i 7 b p 8 t d 9 u q 10 v w

R1.17

KATE Hello. What's your first name, please?

PEDRO It's Pedro.

K What's your surname?

P Molina.

K How do you spell that?

P M–O–L–I–N–A.

K Thank you, Pedro. Welcome to the class.

P Thank you.

R1.18

1

KATE Hello. What's your first name, please?

MAGDA It's Magda.

K How do you spell that?

M M–A–G–D–A.

K Thanks. What's your surname?

M It's Janowska.

K And how do you spell that?

M J–A–N–O–W–S–K–A.

K J–A–N–O–W–S–K–A. Thank you, Magda. Welcome to the class.

M Thank you.

2

KATE Hello. What's your first name, please?

HASAN It's Hasan.

K How do you spell that?

H H–A–S–A–N.

K Thanks. And what's your surname?

H Yousef.

K OK. How do you spell that, please?

H Y–O–U–S–E–F.

K Y–O–U–S–E–F. Thank you, Hasan. Welcome to the class.

H Thank you.

R1.19

first name → What's your first name, please?
surname → What's your surname?
spell that → How do you spell that?

R1.21

1

MAGDA Excuse me.

KATE Yes, Magda?

M What does 'answer' mean?

K I ask a question, you say the answer.

M I'm sorry, I don't understand.

K OK. Question – What's your first name? Answer – It's Magda.

M Oh, OK. I understand. Thank you.

2

PEDRO Excuse me.

KATE Yes, Pedro?

P What's 'lápiz' in English?

K Pencil.

P Can you repeat that, please?

K Pencil.

P Pencil.

K Good.

3

KATE What's the answer to question 1? Pedro?

PEDRO I'm sorry, I don't know.

K Magda?

MAGDA It's Brazil.

K That's right. Good.

HASAN Excuse me. How do you spell 'Brazil'?

K B–R–A–Z–I–L.

H OK. Thank you.

R2.2

ANSWERS A British B Chinese C Brazilian D American

R2.3

I'm → I'm British.
You're → You're a student.
He's → He's Chinese.
She's → She's Brazilian.
It's → It's American.

R2.4

I'm not → I'm not American.
You aren't → You aren't a teacher.
He isn't → He isn't from Beijing.
She isn't → She isn't Australian.
It isn't → It isn't a Mercedes.

R2.6

AMY Ben, do you want to see some photos of my friends?

BEN Sure.

A OK. This is a friend from Germany.

B What's his name?

A Karl. He's a doctor.

B Oh, OK.

A And, um, this is my friend Steve. He's a musician.

B Is he American?

A Yes, he is. He's from Washington. And, er, this is my friend Claire.

B That's a nice photo. Where's she from?

A She's from France. But she's a teacher in London now.

B Really? Hmm. She's beautiful.

A Yes, she is – and she's married.

B Oh.

A And this is my friend Daniela. She's from Italy.

B Is she a musician?

A No, she isn't. She's an actress.

B Oh, OK. Is she married?

A Um, no, she's single.

B Really? What's her phone number?

A Ben!

R2.9

Mr → Mr Brown | Mrs → Mrs King | Ms → Ms King | Ms → Ms Roberts | Miss → Miss Roberts

R2.10

A

RECEPTIONIST Good morning, Mr Brown.

MR BROWN Good morning, Amanda.

B

MR BROWN Good afternoon, Mrs King.

MRS KING Good afternoon.

C

WAITER Good evening, sir.

MR BROWN Good evening.

D

MR BROWN Thank you very much. Good night.

WAITER Good night, sir.

R2.12

at bfl dot com → william dot brown at b f l dot com

at yahoo dot com → frank moon one two three at yahoo dot com

at webmail dot net → anna roberts at webmail dot net

at hotmail dot co dot u k → katy dot king six at hotmail dot co dot u k

R2.13

TONY Good morning. Welcome to the nine2five Employment Agency. My name's Tony.

AMY Nice to meet you.

T You too. OK. First, one or two questions. What's your first name, please?

A It's Amy.

T And what's your surname?

A Foley.

T OK, um, how do you spell that, please?

A F–O–L–E–Y.

T F–O–L–E–Y. Thanks. Are you married?

A No, I'm single.

T And what's your nationality?

A I'm British.

T OK … Right. What's your address?

A It's 9 Whedon Road, Manchester, M11 6JZ.

T How do you spell 'Whedon'?

A W–H–E–D–O–N.

T So that's 9 Whedon Road, Manchester, M11 6JZ.

A Yes, that's right.

T OK, thanks. Right, er, next question. What's your mobile number?

A It's 07866 642339.

T 07866 … er …

A 642339.

T OK, thanks. And what's your email address?

A It's amy.foley@hotmail.co.uk.

T So that's, er, amy.foley@hotmail.co.uk.

A Yes, that's right.

T OK, thanks a lot. Right, um, what kind of job do you want?

R2.14

What's your first name, please?

What's your surname?

Are you married?

What's your nationality?

What's your address?

What's your mobile number?

What's your email address?

R2.19

1

WOMAN 1 Good morning, Tony.

TONY Good morning, Mrs Blake.

W1 Oh is this your cat?

T Yes, his name's Charlie.

W1 How old is he?

T He's thirteen.

2

MAN 1 How old is your house, Tony?

TONY It's a hundred years old, I think.

M1 Oh, right.

3

TONY And this is Emily.

WOMAN 2 Hello, Emily.

EMILY Hello.

W2 How old are you?

E I'm nine.

4

MAN 2 Is that your car?

TONY Yes, it is.

M2 How old is it?

T It's twenty-one years old.

M2 Wow!

5

TONY Bonnie … come here … good girl.

WOMAN 3 What a nice dog. How old is she?

T She's seven. Or forty-nine, in dog years!

R2.20

2 is 3 old 4 are 5 I'm

R3.3

1 We aren't Italian, we're Spanish.

2 You're a very good teacher.

3 They're in a small hotel.

4 He's a doctor and he isn't married.

5 I'm an actor and she's a musician.

6 It's a very old city.

R3.7

1 Nick is Fiona's husband. 2 Kevin is Nick's son. 3 Fiona is Kevin's mother. 4 Anne is Fiona's daughter. 5 Nick is Anne's father. 6 Anne is Kevin's sister. 7 Nick and Fiona are Kevin and Anne's parents.

R3.9

MARY I'm Mary and this is Sid, my husband. I'm 65 and Sid is 64 – like the Beatles song! This is a photo of our daughter Fiona and her family. Fiona's a teacher at a big school in Manchester. She's 43 now, or is it 44?

No, she's 43. Her husband's name is Nick and he's a doctor. And I think he's a very good father.

And these are their two children – our grandchildren. This is Anne, our granddaughter. She's 14, and she's a very good musician. And this is our grandson Kevin. He's 11 – oh no, he's 12 now. It's a very nice photo, I think.

R3.10

ANSWERS 2b) 3e) 4c) 5a) 6d)

R3.11

a) seventeen pounds b) seventy p
c) a hundred dollars d) twenty-one euros
e) thirty-five cents f) twenty-one dollars fifty g) three euros seventy-five h) seven pounds sixty

R3.12

1

A Excuse me. How much is this watch?

B It's twenty-five pounds.

2

A This is very nice. How much is it?

B It's sixty-four dollars.

3

A How much are the pens?

B They're seventy p.

A OK. Two, please.

4

A These bags are beautiful. How much are they?

B They're forty-eight pounds fifty.

A OK, thank you.

5

A They're nice.

B Yes, but they're very expensive.

A How much are they?

B They're ninety-five euros.

A Oh …

R3.14

a coffee | a cappuccino | an espresso | a tea | a mineral water | a Coke | an orange juice | a croissant | an egg sandwich | a cheese and tomato sandwich

R3.15

1

ASSISTANT Can I help you?

CUSTOMER 1 Yes, two cappuccinos, please.

A Sure. Anything else?

C1 Yes. A croissant, please.

A Eat in or take away?

C1 Eat in, please.

A OK, that's … five pounds eighty-five, please.

C1 Thank you very much.

A You're welcome.

Recording Scripts

2

ASSISTANT Hi, can I help you?

CUSTOMER 2 Er, yes, an espresso and an egg sandwich, please.

A Sure. Anything else?

C2 No, that's all, thanks.

A Eat in or take away?

C2 Take away, please.

A OK, that's, um, three pounds seventy-five, please.

C2 Thanks a lot.

A You're welcome.

R3.16

Can I help you?
Yes, two cappuccinos, please.
Sure. Anything else?
Yes, a croissant, please.
No, that's all, thanks.
Eat in or take away?
Eat in, please.
Take away, please.
OK, that's £5.85, please.
Thank you very much.
Thanks a lot.
You're welcome.

R3.19

FIONA What food and drink does my family like? Well, my husband Nick and I like a lot of the same things. We love coffee, but we like it black, not white. And we drink a lot of tea – it's very good for you, they say. And food, well, we don't eat meat, but we eat a lot of fish.
Our children, Anne and Kevin, well, they like eggs, and they eat a lot of pasta. And they're children, so they love chocolate, of course!

R4.4

ANSWERS 2 live 3 have 4 don't have 5 don't live 6 work 7 study 8 like

R4.8

1 Do you go to the cinema?
2 What food do you like?
3 Where do you go shopping?
4 Do you play computer games?

R4.9

Where do you live?
What music do you like?
Do you go to concerts?
Do you like Mexican food?
Do you go to the cinema?
What food do you like?
Where do you go shopping?
Do you play computer games?
Yes, I do.
No, I don't.

R4.11

ANSWERS A £4.75 B 50p C £6.95 D £3.59

R4.12

this → this map → How much is this map?
these → these postcards → How much are these postcards?
that → that box of chocolates → How much is that box of chocolates?
those → those batteries → How much are those batteries?

R4.13

ANSWERS 2 tissues 3 £5.45 4 postcards 5 two 6 £10.65

R4.14

Excuse me.
Do you have any maps of London?
Yes, they're over there.
How much is this map?
It's £4.75.
How much are these postcards?
They're 50p each.
Can I have that box of chocolates, please?
Sure. Anything else?
Yes, this birthday card, please.
No, that's all, thanks.
OK, that's £10.65.
Here you are.
Thanks a lot.
Thanks very much.

R4.18

1

WOMAN Excuse me.

MAN Yes?

W What time is it, please?

M It's twenty to three.

W Thank you.

2

STUDENT Federico?

FEDERICO Yes?

S What time is your English class?

F It's at half past eight.

3

ANNOUNCER And the time is now six o'clock. Here is today's news, read by Graham Robertson.

4

SOPHIE Goodbye, Colin.

COLIN Bye, Sophie. See you at quarter to twelve tomorrow.

S Yes, see you.

5

TEACHER OK, that's it. Thanks a lot. See you on Wednesday at two thirty.

STUDENTS OK. / See you. / Bye. / Cheers. / Thank you.

R5.2

ANSWERS b) 7.45 c) 8.15 d) 9.00 e) 12.45 f) 5.30 g) 6.15 h) 7.30

R5.4

like, likes | play, plays | start, starts | finish, finishes | have, has | study, studies | love, loves | go, goes | eat, eats | watch, watches | drink, drinks | read, reads

R5.6

TOM Here you are, Carol. A cheese sandwich and a cappuccino.

CAROL Thanks a lot, Tom. Oh look, there's Nadine!

T Who's Nadine?

C She works in the mobile phone shop with me. Nadine! Hi!

NADINE Hello, Carol! How are you?

C I'm fine, thanks. Nadine, this is my brother Tom.

N Nice to meet you, Tom.

T You too. So, um, you work in the mobile phone shop with Carol.

N Yes, that's right. But I don't work in the week, only at the weekend.

T What do you do in the week?

N I'm a student at the university. I study English and Italian.

T Oh, OK. Where are you from?

N I'm from Germany. From Frankfurt.

T And where do you live in Manchester?

N I live near the university with two other students.

C Do you like Manchester?

N Yes, I do. The people are nice and there are a lot of things to do here.

T What do you do in your free time?

N I play tennis and, er, I go to the cinema a lot. And what about you, Tom? Are you a student?

T No, I'm a waiter. I work in a restaurant called the New Moon.

N Oh yes, I know it. It's in Cross Street, isn't it?

R5.9

chicken salad | vegetable lasagne | burger and chips | mushroom pizza | apple pie and cream | fruit salad | chocolate ice cream | strawberry ice cream | vanilla ice cream | a bottle of mineral water | still | sparkling | a Coke | an orange juice | a coffee | a tea

R5.17

Listening Test (see Teacher's Book)

R6.3

ANSWERS 2 are 3 's 4 are 5 's 6 are 7 's 8 are

R6.5

SUSAN Well, here we are, Isabel. Come in. Welcome to my home.

ISABEL Thanks, Susan. Oh, what a beautiful flat!

S Thanks a lot.

I Do you like living here?

s Yes, I do. It's a nice road and the people are very friendly.

I That's good. Are there any shops near here?

s Yes, there are. In this road there's, um, a small supermarket, a chemist's and a post office.

I Is there a bank?

s No, there isn't. But there's a cashpoint at the post office. And there are a lot of banks in the centre of Bath, of course.

I OK. Are we near the city centre?

s Yes, it's only two miles from here.

I Oh, right. And can I get to the centre by train?

s No, there isn't a station near here, but, um, there are buses to the city centre every ten minutes. The bus stop's near the post office.

I That's good to know. And what about places to eat?

s Well, there aren't any good restaurants near here, but, um, there are some very nice restaurants in the centre.

I Great! Maybe we can go out for dinner this evening.

s Yes, that's a good idea. Right, this is your room …

R6.7

There's an expensive market.
There are some old buildings.
There isn't an airport.
There aren't any museums.
Is there a post office?
Yes, there is.
No, there isn't.
Are there any nice old cafés?
Yes, there are.
No, there aren't.

R6.9

1

ISABEL Good morning.

ASSISTANT Hello. Can I help you?

I Yes, please. Do you have a map of the city centre?

A Yes, of course. Here you are.

I Thank you. How much is it?

A It's a pound.

I Oh, OK. Here you are. Thank you very much.

2

ASSISTANT Hello. Can I help you?

TOURIST 1 Er, yes, please. When is the Roman Baths Museum open?

A It's open from 9 a.m. to 5 p.m.

T1 Is it closed on Mondays?

A No, it's open every day.

T1 Thanks a lot.

3

TOURIST 2 Good morning.

ASSISTANT Hello. Can I help you?

T2 Yes, please. Where's the Thermae Bath Spa?

A It's in Hot Bath Street.

T2 Can you show me on this map?

A Yes, of course. Here it is. It's about five minutes away.

T2 Thank you very much.

R6.10

Good morning.
Hello. Can I help you?
Yes, please.
Do you have a map of the city centre?
Yes, of course. Here you are.
Thank you. How much is it?
It's a pound.
When is the Roman Baths Museum open?
It's open from nine a.m. to five p.m.
Is it closed on Mondays?
No, it's open every day.
Where's the Thermae Bath Spa?
It's in Hot Bath Street.
Can you show me on this map?
Yes, of course. Here it is.
It's about five minutes away.
Thank you very much.

R6.11

ANSWERS 2 of 3 Here you are. 4 is it 5 It's
6 afternoon 7 is 8 from 9 to 10 Is it
11 day 12 help 13 Where's 14 in 15 map
16 Here it is.

R6.14

LISA My favourite colour is pink and this is my favourite dress. I love this coat too, and these shoes. I have about … about thirty pairs of shoes at home, but I never wear trainers. I don't think they look good on girls.

BRAD I usually wear jeans, a T-shirt and, um, these trainers. My clothes are usually blue or black, and I never wear brown. Oh, and this is my favourite jacket, this black one. It's about five years old and I love it!

WAYNE I love shopping for clothes and I have about ten suits at home. I always wear a suit and tie for work, and, er, this is my favourite shirt, this blue one. But I never wear jeans. They don't look good on me.

MONICA I usually wear a skirt for work, like today, and I love wearing jumpers when it's cold. And these are my favourite boots. I wear them all the time. But, um, but I never wear dresses. I don't like them.

R6.15

My favourite colour is pink.
This is my favourite jacket.
These are my favourite boots.
What's your favourite colour?
Who's your favourite actor?

R7.3

1

A Do you like dancing?

B Yes, I love it.

2

A Do you like Madonna?

B Yes, I like her a lot.

3

A Do you like shopping for clothes?

B No, I hate it.

4

A Do you like Johnny Depp?

B Yes, I love him.

5

A Do you like soap operas?

B No, I hate them.

6

A Do you like dogs?

B Yes, but they don't like me!

R7.6

1 I can play the guitar. 2 You can't cook.
3 He can play basketball. 4 She can't drive.
5 We can't speak French. 6 They can sing very well.

R7.7

MRS JONES Hello, Maria. My name's Patricia Jones. Nice to meet you.

MARIA You too.

MRS J Right, we want an au pair to help us with our two children, Ella and Daniel.

M OK. How old are they?

MRS J Ella's eleven and Daniel's nine.

M Right.

MRS J So, I have some questions if that's OK.

M Of course.

MRS J Can you cook?

M Yes, I can. I love cooking. I often cook dinner for my family at home.

MRS J That's good. Can you drive?

M Yes, I can.

MRS J OK, great. And can you speak German or French?

M Um, I can't speak German … but I can speak French well.

MRS J Oh, great. The children both study French. And what about free time activities? Can you swim?

M Yes, I can.

MRS J And can you play tennis?

M No, I can't. Sorry. I don't like sport very much.

MRS J That's OK. What about music? Can you play the piano?

M No, I can't. But I can sing and I can play the guitar.

MRS J Oh, that's good. Daniel plays the guitar too. Maybe you can help him.
M Yes, of course.
MRS J OK, one last question.
M Yes, Mrs Jones?
MRS J When can you start?

R7.10

ANSWERS 2 museum 3 museum 4 bank 5 bank

R7.11

Excuse me. Where's the museum?
Excuse me. Is there a bank near here?
Go along this road and turn left.
Go along this road and turn right.
That's Park Street.
The museum is on the right, next to the theatre.
The bank is on the left, opposite the station.
It's over there, near the cinema.

R7.12

ANSWERS 2 here 3 right 4 on 5 near 6 Where's 7 over 8 next to 9 near 10 along 11 right 12 hotel

R7.13

send emails | receive emails | buy concert tickets | buy theatre tickets | watch videos | watch TV programmes | listen to the radio | chat to friends | chat to family | buy things | sell things | book flights | book holidays | download music

R7.14

INTERVIEWER Excuse me?
ALICE Yes?
I Can I ask you some questions about the Internet?
A Yes, sure.
I Thanks very much. OK, do you send and receive emails?
A Yes, of course. I get a hundred emails a day at work!
I Right. And do you buy concert or theatre tickets online?
A Yes, I do.
I OK. Do you watch videos or TV programmes on the Internet?
A Yes, all the time. I love YouTube. It's my favourite website.
I OK, thanks. And what about the radio? Do you listen to the radio online?
A Er, no, I don't.
I Do you chat to friends or family online?
A Yes, sometimes. My sister lives in New York and we chat online every week.
I OK. Do you buy and sell things online?
A Yes, I buy DVDs on Amazon and sell them again on eBay.
I And do you book flights or holidays online?

A No, I don't. My husband always does that.
I OK, the last question. Do you download music from the Internet?
A No, I don't. I don't have an iPod.
I OK, thanks very much, that's great.
A No problem. Bye.

R8.3

I was at the World Cup Final.
We were near the Opera House.
The stadium wasn't full.
They weren't very happy.
I was very young at the time.
It was a great match!
It was a fantastic New Year!
There were some amazing fireworks!
The concert wasn't very long.

R8.6

FRIEND Rajeet, are you busy on Saturday?
RAJEET Yes, I am, sorry. It's my wedding anniversary.
F Oh, happy anniversary!
R Thanks a lot. It's amazing that my wedding was ten years ago.
F Was it in London?
R No, it wasn't. It was in Mumbai, in India.
F Really?
R Yes. Gita was born in the UK, but her father's parents live in Mumbai.
F And how old were you on your wedding day?
R I was 34 and Gita was 27.
F Oh. Was it a big wedding?
R Yes, it was. There were three hundred people there.
F Oh, wow! Were all your family at the wedding?
R No, they weren't. My brother was in Australia, so he wasn't there. (Oh.) But my parents and my two sisters were there.
F And was there a party after the wedding?
R Yes, there was – for three days!
F Three days?! That's amazing!
R Yes, there was fantastic Indian food and a lot of dancing. I was very tired at the end!
F I'm sure you were. So what are your plans for Saturday?

R8.7

Where was the wedding?
How old were Rajeet and Gita?
How many people were at the wedding?
Where was Rajeet's brother?
Was he at the wedding?
Yes, he was.
No, he wasn't.
Were they at the wedding?
Yes, they were.
No, they weren't.
Where was Gita born?
She was born in the UK.
When were you born?
I was born in nineteen eighty seven.

R8.12

1
A What's the date today?
B It's June 22nd.
A Thanks a lot.

2
A When's your birthday?
B March 30th.
A Really? That's my birthday too!

3
A When's your wedding anniversary?
B It's on October 3rd.
A Oh, that's next week.

4
A When do you start your new job?
B On April 1st.
A Really? Er … good luck!

R8.13

SAM Happy birthday! Twenty-one again!
HELEN Thanks a lot.
S Here's a present for you.
H Ooh, thank you. Oh, what an amazing dress! It's a beautiful colour too. Oh, thanks, Sam. I love it.
S I'm pleased you like it. So, what shall we do this evening?
H Oh, I don't know. Do you have any good ideas?
S Let's have dinner at your favourite restaurant.
H You mean Antonio's? No, I don't think so. We were there a week ago.
S Yes, OK. Why don't we go to the cinema?
H Maybe, but we go to the cinema every week.
S Hmm. I know! Let's go to the theatre. We never do that.
H Yes, that's a good idea. Do you know what's on?
S Well, there's a new play on at the Grand Theatre. People say that it's very good.
H Great! Let's go to that. Where shall we meet?
S Let's meet at the theatre. It's in Old Street, near the museum.
H Oh yes, I know where it is. What time shall we meet?
S About seven o'clock. Then we can have a drink first.
H Yes, good idea.
S Right, time to go. See you this evening, birthday girl!
H Bye. Have a good day.

R8.14

What shall we do this evening?
Why don't we go to the cinema?
Let's go to the theatre.
Yes, that's a good idea.

Maybe.
No, I don't think so.
Where shall we meet?
Let's meet at the theatre.
What time shall we meet?
About seven o'clock.

R8.15

GEORGE What shall we do tomorrow evening, Jessica?

JESSICA Why don't we go to the cinema?

G No, I don't think so.

J OK. Let's go to that Indian restaurant in Old Street.

G Yes, that's a good idea. Where shall we meet?

J Let's meet at the restaurant.

G OK. What time shall we meet?

J About quarter to eight.

G Great! See you there!

R8.17

a) three hundred and sixty-five b) nine hundred and ninety-nine c) seventeen thousand d) sixty-two thousand, four hundred e) two hundred and fifty thousand f) one million, two hundred thousand g) eighteen million

R8.18

a) 30,000 b) 125,000 c) 150,000 d) 1,500 e) 177,500 f) 70,000,000

R9.2

visit, visited | watch, watched | play, played | hate, hated | walk, walked | work, worked | live, lived | want, wanted | love, loved | talk, talked | start, started | finish, finished

R9.5

1 I liked your photos. I like your photos.
2 We live in Spain. We lived in Spain.
3 They arrived at ten. They arrive at ten.
4 We talk every day. We talked every day.
5 I want to go home. I wanted to go home.
6 They played football a lot. They play football a lot.

R9.10

CAROLINE Hello, James. Did you have a good weekend?

JAMES Hi, Caroline. Yes, I did, thanks. I didn't go out, I stayed at home all weekend and watched TV. What about you? What did you do?

C Paul and I went to Liverpool.

J Oh, great! Did you have a good time?

C Yes, we did. It's a very interesting city with some beautiful buildings.

J What did you do there?

C Well, um, on Saturday we walked around the city and I took a lot of photos. And in the evening we went out for dinner at a very nice Chinese restaurant.

J Did you stay in a hotel?

C No, we didn't. Paul's sister lives in Liverpool, so we stayed with her.

J And what did you do on Sunday?

C Well, er, in the morning we visited the Beatles museum. Then in the afternoon we went to the Cavern Club, where the Beatles first played. That was amazing!

J Wow! Did you go to Liverpool by train?

C Yes, we did. It's only three hours from London.

J Really?

C Yes, why don't you go sometime?

J Yes, maybe. It's, um, my wife's birthday next weekend and we don't have any plans.

C Hey, look at the time! We're late for work!

R9.12 **R9.13**

Two returns to Liverpool, please.
When do you want to come back?
Tomorrow evening.
OK. That's ninety-three pounds forty, please.
Here are your tickets.
Thanks. What time's the next train?
There's one at nine seventeen.
Which platform?
Platform six.
What time does it arrive in Liverpool?
At twelve twenty-nine.
Thanks a lot. Bye.

R9.14

ANSWERS 2 That's 3 your 4 next 5 at 6 Which 7 does 8 At 9 a lot

R10.5

WESLEY Hello, Liam.

LIAM Hi, Wesley.

W Busy day?

L Yes, Mondays are always busy. You?

W Yes, we had a lot of new customers today. And it's going to be difficult without Darla.

L What do you mean?

W Don't you know? Darla's going to move to Australia next month.

L Australia?! Really?

DARLA Yes, this is my last week at the bank.

L Wow! I didn't know that. Why Australia?

D My husband, Justin, is going to work for a travel company there.

L OK. And what about you? What are you going to do?

D I don't know. I'm going to look for a job when I arrive.

W Are you going to sell your flat in London?

D No, we're not. My two sisters are going to live there.

L That's a good idea. Are you going to have a party before you leave?

D No, but Justin and I are going to have dinner with some friends in a restaurant next Saturday. You know, to say goodbye. Er, would you like to come, Liam?

L Oh, yes, please. Um, thanks very much.

D Great. Wesley's going to be there, of course.

L Oh … er … maybe I'm busy on Saturday.

W Ha ha, very funny!

L Anyway, I'm going to go to the cinema this evening. Do you want to come?

W Maybe. What are you going to see?

L Well, it's called …

R10.6

1 What are you going to do next weekend?
2 What are you going to do after class?
3 When are you going to do your homework?
4 What time are you going to get up tomorrow?
5 Where are you going to have dinner tomorrow evening?
6 Where are you going to go on holiday next year?

R10.8

ANSWERS 2 holiday 3 two 4 course 5 September 6 job 7 exam 8 day

R10.9

Have a good holiday!
Thanks a lot.
Have a good journey!
Have a good day!
Have a good weekend!
Have a good birthday!
Have a good time!
See you in September.
Yes, see you.
See you in two weeks.
See you next month.
See you on Monday.
Good luck with your exam.
Thanks very much.
Good luck with your new job.
Good luck with your English test.
Good luck with your new school.

R10.10

A

ALAN What are you going to do after work?

KERRY I'm going to have dinner with friends.

A Have a good time!

K Thanks a lot.

A See you tomorrow.

K Yes, see you. Bye!

B

SID I'm going to go on holiday next week.

JAN Really? Where are you going?

S To Bodrum, in Turkey.

J Have a good holiday!

S Thanks. Oh, and good luck with your new job.

J Thanks a lot.

R10.11

Listening Test (see Teacher's Book)

125

Phonemic Symbols

Vowel sounds

/ə/	/æ/	/ʊ/	/ɒ/	/ɪ/	/i/	/e/	/ʌ/
c<u>o</u>mput<u>e</u>r	b<u>a</u>g m<u>a</u>n	b<u>oo</u>k g<u>oo</u>d	c<u>o</u>ffee h<u>o</u>t	s<u>i</u>x th<u>i</u>ng	happ<u>y</u> eas<u>y</u>	b<u>e</u>d <u>a</u>ny	m<u>u</u>ch s<u>o</u>n

/ɜː/	/ɑː/	/uː/	/ɔː/	/iː/			
b<u>ur</u>ger g<u>ir</u>l	f<u>a</u>ther c<u>ar</u>	bl<u>ue</u> wh<u>o</u>	f<u>or</u>ty w<u>a</u>ter	<u>ea</u>t m<u>ee</u>t			

/eə/	/ɪə/	/ʊə/	/ɔɪ/	/aɪ/	/eɪ/	/əʊ/	/aʊ/
ch<u>air</u> wh<u>ere</u>	n<u>ear</u> w<u>e're</u>	t<u>ou</u>rist	b<u>oy</u> n<u>oi</u>sy	n<u>i</u>ne m<u>y</u>	<u>eigh</u>t d<u>ay</u>	g<u>o</u> kn<u>ow</u>	<u>ou</u>t br<u>ow</u>n

Consonant sounds

/p/	/b/	/f/	/v/	/t/	/d/	/k/	/g/
<u>p</u>ark sho<u>p</u>	<u>b</u>e <u>b</u>ike	<u>f</u>ive le<u>f</u>t	<u>v</u>ery li<u>v</u>e	<u>t</u>ime whi<u>t</u>e	<u>d</u>og re<u>d</u>	<u>c</u>old loo<u>k</u>	<u>g</u>irl ba<u>g</u>

/θ/	/ð/	/tʃ/	/dʒ/	/s/	/z/	/ʃ/	/ʒ/
<u>th</u>ree <u>th</u>ink	mo<u>th</u>er <u>th</u>e	<u>ch</u>ips mu<u>ch</u>	<u>o</u>range <u>j</u>uice	<u>s</u>uit <u>c</u>ity	<u>z</u>ero day<u>s</u>	<u>sh</u>irt <u>s</u>ugar	televi<u>s</u>ion

/m/	/n/	/ŋ/	/h/	/l/	/r/	/w/	/j/
<u>m</u>e na<u>m</u>e	<u>n</u>ow trai<u>n</u>	si<u>ng</u> thi<u>nk</u>	<u>h</u>ere <u>h</u>ello	<u>l</u>eave p<u>l</u>ane	<u>r</u>ead p<u>r</u>ice	<u>w</u>aiter <u>w</u>e	<u>y</u>ou <u>y</u>es

Answer Key

1D ❼ p98

3 tables; 5 men; 2 women; 10 books; 3 pens; 8 pencils; 7 apples; 4 bags; 6 mobiles

2A ❾ b) p15

3 Cameron Diaz isn't Spanish. She's American.
4 ✓
5 ✓
6 Big Ben isn't in New York. It's in London.
7 Kylie Minogue isn't American. She's Australian.
8 Robbie Williams isn't an Australian singer. He's a British singer.
9 ✓
10 Hollywood isn't in San Francisco. It's in Los Angeles.

2D ❿ p98

Maria 45; Mary 76; Christopher 70; John 65; Chris 46; Stef 43; Martin 38; Adela 41; Alex 37; Lola 1; Freddie 8; Dagmar 72; Maja 6; Lily 3

9D ❶ c) p76

1c) 2b) 3a) 4a) 5c) 6a) 7b) 8c)

Classroom Instructions

Listen.

Read.

Write.

Look at the photo.

Work in pairs.

Work in groups.

Match.

Fill in the gaps.

Compare answers.

Listen and check.

Listen and practise.

Ask and answer the questions.

CD-ROM/Audio CD Instructions

Start the CD-ROM

- Insert the *face2face* CD-ROM into your CD-ROM drive.
- If Autorun is enabled, the CD-ROM will start automatically.
- If Autorun is not enabled, open **My Computer** and then **D:** (where D is the letter of your CD-ROM drive). Then double-click on the *face2face* icon.

Install the CD-ROM to your hard disk (recommended)

- Go to **My Computer** and then **D:** (where D is the letter of your CD-ROM drive).
- Right-click on *Explore*.
- Double-click on *Install face2face to hard disk*.
- Follow the installation instructions on your screen.

Listen and practise on your CD player

You can listen to and practise language from the Student's Book Real World lessons on your CD player at home or in the car:
R1.19 R1.22 R2.12 R2.14 R3.10 R3.13 R3.16 R4.14
R5.11 R6.10 R7.11 R8.11 R8.14 R9.13 R10.9

What's on the CD-ROM?

- **Interactive practice activities**
Extra practice of Grammar, Vocabulary, Real World situations and English pronunciation. Click on one of the unit numbers (1–10) at the top of the screen. Then choose an activity and click on it to start.

- **My Activities**
Create your own lesson. Click on *My Activities* at the top of the screen. Drag activities from the unit menus into the *My Activities* panel on the right of the screen. Then click on *Start*.

- **My Portfolio**
This is a unique and customisable reference tool. Click on *Grammar, Word List, Real World* or *Phonemes* at any time for extra help and information. You can also add your own notes, check your progress and create your own English tests!

Practice activities | My Activities | My Portfolio

System specification
- Windows XP or Vista
- 256MB RAM for XP, 1GB for Vista
- 500MB hard disk space (if installing to hard disk)

Support
If you experience difficulties with this CD-ROM, please email:
cdrom@cambridge.org

Acknowledgements

Chris Redston would like to thank all at Cambridge University Press for their continuing support, energy and dedication to the *face2face* project, in particular: Sue Ullstein (Freelance editor), Ruth Atkinson (Freelance editor), Karen Momber (Commissioning Editor), Dilys Silva (Senior Development Editor), Ian Collier (Electronic Project Manager), Nikolaos Kovaios (Electronic Project Developer), Nicholas Tims and Alison Greenwood (CD-ROM team) and all the team at pentacor**big** (Design).

The author would also like to thank the following people for their support: Mark Skipper, Heidi Sowter, Will Ord, Margie Fisher, Laura Jansen, Dylan Evans, Mat and Sarah Hunt, Braw Innes, Natasha Muñoz, Steve Moore, Emma Murphy, Jean Barmer, Mary Breen, Anitha Mõdig, Chris and Dagmar Pickles, Joss Whedon, JJ Abrams, the Hilder family, the Ghosh family, his dear sisters, Anne and Carol, and his father, Bill Redston (see, I do get out of bed occasionally, Dad!). Particular thanks go to his two editors, Sue Ullstein and Ruth Atkinson, for being such wonderful people to work with, and to Gillie Cunningham, for all her help and support since we started writing *face2face* together. Finally, he would like to offer very special thanks to Adela Pickles for her patience, encouragement and love while book-writing guy does his thing. Fun-loving guy will take you to see some lemurs now. You!

The author and publishers would like to thank the following teachers for the invaluable feedback which they provided:

Norma Alburquerque, Peru; Isidro Almendárez, Spain; Steve Banfield, UAE; Tom Bolton, Ecuador; Liliana Burgos, Peru; Consuelo Cedano, Colombia / UK; Lois Clegg, Italy; Kate Cory-Wright, Mexico; Amalia de la Bastida, Ecuador; Lucie Fischerová, Czech Republic; Sausen Hassanbek, Libya; Jan Peter Isaksen, Mexico; Helen Paul, Germany; Johanna Stirling, UK; Wayne Trotman, Turkey; Dawn Van den Berg, UK; Lawrence Wang, Taiwan; Sue Watson, Libya

The author and publishers are grateful to the following contributors:

pentacor**big**: cover and text design and page make-up
Hilary Luckcock: picture research, commissioned photography
Trevor Clifford: photography
Anne Rosenfeld: audio recordings

The publishers are grateful to the following for permission to reproduce copyright photographs and material:

Key: l = left, c = centre, r = right, t = top, b = bottom

Alamy Images/©Peter Treanor for p14(D), /©Ken Walsh for p15(1), /©vario images GmbH & Co. KG for p15(4), /©vario images GmbH & Co. KG for p15(9), /©Tetra Images for p17(1), /©Photogenix for p23(l), ©Melvyn Longhurst for p30, /©William Caram for p31, /©BlueMoon Stock for p63(bl), /©Jon Arnold Images Ltd for p73(t), /©Ian Pilbeam for p74(bl), /©naglestock.com for p76(moon), /©The Print Collector for p76(Titanic), /©The London Art Archive for p76(Columbus), /©TS Corrigan for p76(Everest), /©Rubberball for p91(Daniel), /©Photogenix for p94(tl), /©Rubberball for p97(Daniel); Bath Tourism Plus for p46 and 47; Cheapflights.co.uk for p60; Corbis/©Stephane Reix/For Picture for p9(1), /©Peter Andrews for p9(2), /©Camilla Morandi for 9(4), /©George Tiedemann for p15(2), /©Claro Cortes IV/Reuters for p15(3),